The
Unself-
Help Book

The Unself-Help Book

How to Get Out of Your Own Way and Start **Being Happy**

CARL T. VREELAND

LAUER BOOKS LLC

NEW ROCHELLE, NY

Lauer Books LLC, February 2026
New Rochelle, NY

Cover design: Kam Bains
Interior design: Iram Allam

Library of Congress Control Number: 2025921934
ISBN: 979-8-9934133-1-0

Printed in the USA.

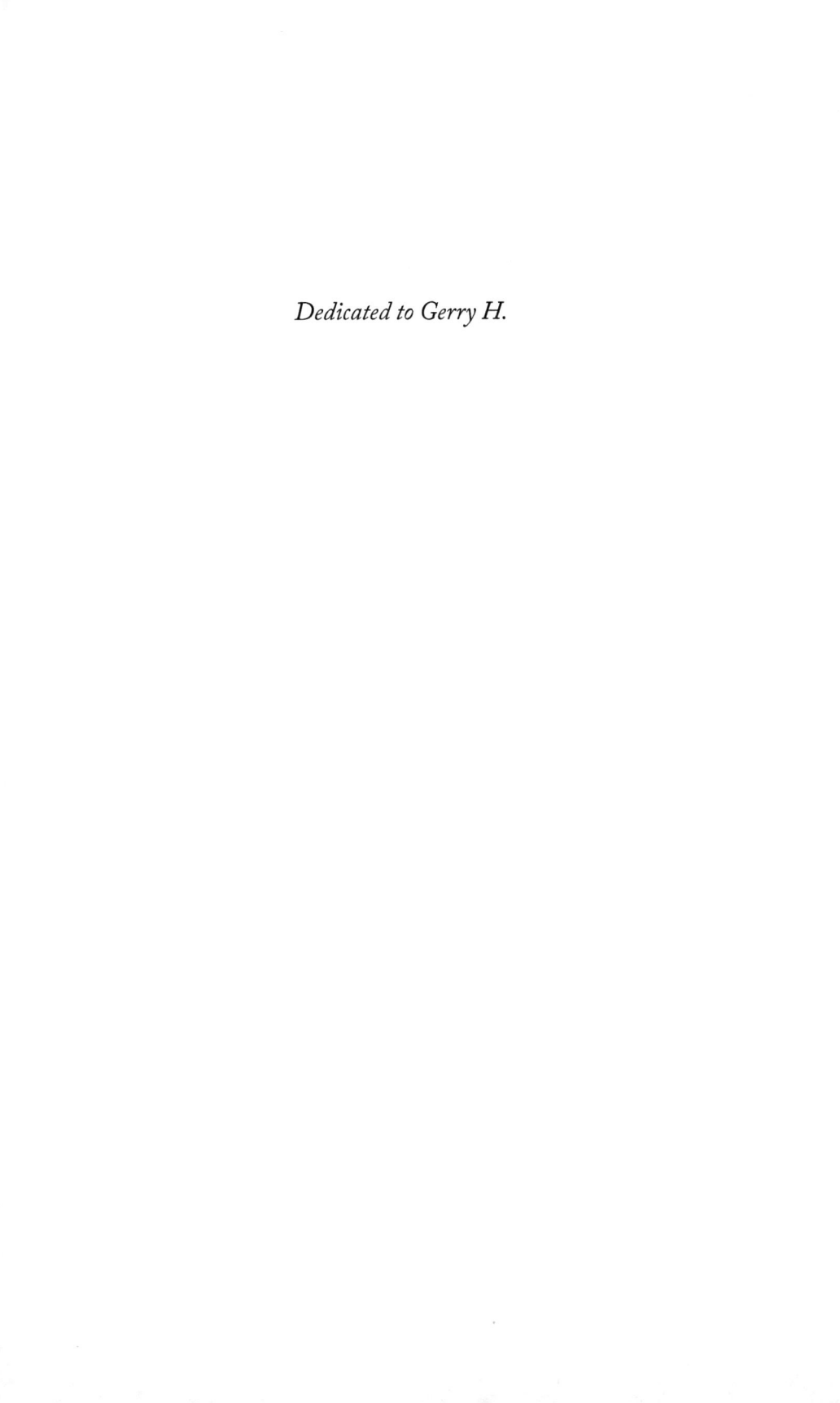

Dedicated to Gerry H.

To "unself" refers to the act of removing oneself from a rigid focus on the self and ridding oneself of self-centeredness. In essence, unselfing promotes a deflation of the ego so as to deepen one's connection with others and the world.

Contents

Introduction

I was finished. I lay there in the dark, terribly broken and sleep-deprived. After many months of wakeful nights, writhing, weeping, and bellowing, a silence and a stillness settled over me. I collapsed in my bed, on my back, arms stretched out to the sides like a supine cross, crucified. Turning to something greater than me, I raised my hand and softly cried, "I surrender. I am done. Take my hand, God; lead the way." I let go of all my expectations and hopes. Released, my body, mind, and spirit slowly drifted into a deep, heavy sleep.

Hours passed, and the sun rose. It was quiet. I opened my eyes and noticed my breath. The air was crisp. Everything seemed strange, foreign, and otherworldly. The room was quiet and peaceful, as was the world outside my window. Everything had changed. My life, as I knew it, was over.

Before going deeply into what happened, I want to set up my story and why I am writing this book. I was an active alcoholic. And in short, it was my alcoholism that led me to a place of surrender and serenity. But this story is not simply about a drunk who gets sober, finds peace of mind, and turns his life around. This book is about how adversity can lead to astonishing transformations, whether our suffering stems from alcoholism, betrayal, divorce, disillusionment, depression, the death of a loved one, or some other setback or hardship.

I came to realize that nothing on the outside was going to relieve me of my inner turmoil and feelings of emptiness and alienation. Over time, I learned that happiness is an inside job. Just as important, I discovered that alcoholics and addicts don't corner the market on suffering; it's a condition we all experience. It's called the human condition.

I found an alternative way of living. Unlike the self-help methods I'd exhausted, and beyond the insights and lessons I'd learned in talk therapy, this new model of living profoundly changed my core *being*. It revealed to me my true self by helping me see outside my *self*. It helped me curtail my self-centeredness, selfishness, and self-absorption. In essence, it enabled me to *unself*.

The wisdom I came upon goes beyond self-analysis, self-help, and New Age affirmations that promise happiness and success yet leave many of us unfulfilled and dissatisfied. The following pages present a more grounded, practical approach to life that asks us to stop searching for happiness and to start focusing on the causes of our suffering. More than that, the book details, by way of narrative, each significant step I took in my struggle to unearth the causes of my suffering and to overcome depression, alcoholism, addiction, hopelessness, and an overall dissatisfaction with life.

In my sobriety, while cultivating a spiritual way of living and helping others in recovery, I dug deeply into the contemplative practices. This led me to leave behind a thirty-year career as a touring musician and singer/songwriter. I traded in a life of drugs, sex, and rock 'n' roll for a sane, sober, and spiritual one. I started teaching Yoga and Buddhist meditation, sharing the knowledge I had learned. I developed close relationships with many of my students who took a strong interest in what I had to offer, and I became part of a community of fellow teachers and seekers.

I believe the wisdom in this book has the potential to profoundly change your life for the better. Whether you're an alcoholic or not, whether you have addiction issues or not, whether you're depressed or heartbroken—regardless of the causes of your suffering, I hope the following pages guide you onto your path of healing, happiness, and peace.

CHAPTER ONE

Happiness: An Alternative View

Why is happiness so elusive for many of us?
Why does our endless search for it seem futile?

I just wanted to be happy. In fact, I spent much of my time and energy searching for happiness. Like many of us, I was drawn to motivating adages, such as "Do what makes you happy." "Choose happiness." "You deserve to be happy." I read the books, viewed the videos, and attended the seminars and classes that offered me the promise of a happy life. Yet the authors, self-help gurus, and celebrity motivational speakers who claimed to have discovered the secrets to achieving happiness did not help me.

Our preoccupation with happiness has become so significant that the promise of it has turned into a strong marketing strategy. Pharmaceutical companies, plastic surgeons, and diet programs pledge to give us a happier life, and we sincerely want to believe their sales pitches. "My psychiatrist informed me that this new drug will lift my spirits." "As soon as I save up enough money for my breast implants, I will be confident again." "I just need to lose twenty pounds, then I will feel sexy and appealing." Dating apps, car companies, and real estate agencies guarantee us a better life too. "When the right person comes into my life everything will come together." "When I get a nicer car, I'll be happier." "Once I find my dream home, I'll be able to relax and enjoy my life and the kids."

We are led to believe that happiness can be found by creating the correct conditions. Even if it were true, external conditions are always in flux. Inevitably someone or something will disrupt or disappoint us and happiness will slip out of our hands once again. The person we fell head over heels for will eventually hurt us. Over time we will get bored with our nicer car. And our new noisy neighbors will turn our dream home into a nightmare.

Why is happiness so elusive for many of us? Why does our endless search for it seem futile? Our troubles may seem like they're coming from somewhere on the outside, but they are usually not. "My happiness is out of reach because I hate my job." "I will be happy again once I get a divorce." These observations may or may not be true. Outside of that, those kinds of changes may just be another temporary fix.

Perhaps our pursuit is misdirected. What if we were to shift our focus? What if we were to stop searching for happiness? What if we were to investigate the causes of our unhappiness and seek ways to suffer less instead?

What is behind our brief show of frustration toward our children while running late for work in the morning? What is the energy that fuels the short spell of impatience toward the slow-moving cashier and the slight annoyance for the train being delayed? What is the underlying reason we get angry toward our colleagues for being unprepared? Why do we snap at our mother over the phone for being long-winded, or lose our cool at the lunch counter over a wrong order, or fight with our partner because they forgot to pick up the milk on the way home from work?

I suggest we get honest and start looking at ourselves. But this can be difficult when we feel like we are who we are. "I can't help it; it's just the way I am" is a justification many of us use for our less desirable attributes. "I'm hot-tempered." "I'm sensitive and easily hurt." "I don't handle conflict very well." These traits become our identity, our story, and the narrative we rehearse and refine. We cement these features into our cerebrum, and they become our character qualities, or, more accurately, our character flaws.

Some of us convince ourselves that these traits are virtuous. "I'm a people pleaser; I can't help myself." "I have high standards and so I have high expectations of myself and others." We cleverly claim virtue to avoid facing the truth that they may not be noble qualities.

Likely our shortcomings have more of an impact on our lives than we are willing to admit. In fact, I am convinced that they are among the many causes of our suffering. All the same, our suffering stems from an internal issue—perhaps a deep craving for something more.

The surest way to know if we are the source of our own suffering is by taking care of the inside stuff first. When it comes to making decisions in life, we can't be sure we are making the right ones if we are frustrated, angry, fearful, or feeling empty inside. Our inner wisdom is unable to nudge and guide us in the direction that best suits us when we are not in tune with it.

Opening My Eyes

My drinking problem, my rock bottom, was my rite of passage. It was the universe's way of pushing me to seek help and look within. It was my wake-up call. Not unlike the cancer survivor who comes to know how precious life is, or the prison inmate on death row who finds Jesus, or the soldier who makes it home from the front line in one piece filled with gratitude—alcoholism was my near-death experience—an occurrence that brought down the walls of denial, opened my eyes, let the light in, and guided me. It was my inner compass, my star of Bethlehem, my pathway home.

I had no choice in the matter; it was a life-or-death situation. I had to get sober. But more than that, I had to dig deeper in order to stay sober. I had to face my fears, flaws, and behaviors and find help outside of myself. Now, if we were to get honest about it, without a strong reason, how many of us would willingly dig deeper? It's not easy to do. And why do it if we are relatively content, even if we aren't happy? Well, there's no reason to, unless, of course, something happens—something that causes heartache, hurt, discontentment, anxiety, or immense pain. Still, even under duress and burdensome pain, many of us would rather try to find some form of escape than to look within. That is, until one day our carefully designed plan of escape—pills, alcohol, sex, porn, gambling, shopping sprees, whatever our drug of choice may be—loses its efficacy. That's when our long run as a fugitive fleeing from the hurt comes to an end and our starving soul pins us down and grabs us by the throat. As for me, my body, mind, and spirit shouted, "Enough!" Indeed, the scheme was revealed. Luckily, the universe sent me a gift.

He was seated at the head of a long, off-white, collapsible banquet table. He sported a clean-shaven head with an unidentifiable tattoo on top. The tattoo was about the size of an egg, yet it resembled a sliced half of an avocado. My guess was that it was sexual in nature, likely a vulva. He wore a neatly trimmed Fu Manchu and soul patch. Some call this combo a "Frank Zappa beard," only it was much thinner and the tips of the moustache were silver. But what stood out most were the dangling SpongeBob earrings that hung from each ear, accenting his gold wire-rimmed glasses. He was the chairperson running a recovery meeting in a space called the Serenity Club.

He settled into his seat, set up his papers, and opened the meeting. He introduced himself and read through the guidelines and format for the meeting. Afterward, he briefly told his story. His stunning resurrection from a rare, incurable bone disease; alcoholism; and drug addiction seemed nothing short of miraculous. I was immediately taken by his account and his conviction and charisma. He was vibrant and carried an enthusiasm that demanded unwavering attention. He spoke with confidence yet with humility and without a scratch of self-deprecation. He powerfully projected every word from his heart, and his thorough knowledge and understanding of the recovery program flowed out of him naturally and eloquently. He conveyed a compelling belief in God. He possessed something that I found fascinating but couldn't quite pinpoint, qualities unlike anything I had ever witnessed in a person. Perhaps it was his unaffected positive attitude. Maybe it was his observable genuine desire to help others. Whatever it was, it was palpable. Little did I know that this man would soon save my life. His name: Gerry H.

Stop Searching for Happiness

Gerry frequently said, "Happiness is an inside job" (a quote often attributed to William Arthur Ward). Rather than trying to change our external circumstances, we must change our internal outlook. When we can accept that happiness cannot be attained through possessions, accomplishments, relationships, or anything external—that it's an inside job—we will suffer less. The outside stuff will look and feel different once we take care of the inside stuff. And we'll experience what we truly want: in short, transcendence.

Spiritual teacher and writer Anthony de Mello affirms that "Happiness is our natural state. ... To acquire happiness you don't have to do anything, because happiness cannot be acquired. ... How can you acquire what you already have?"[1] Indeed, happiness is within us, and our emotional and psychological suffering cover it up. When we suffer less, happiness surfaces. It emerges from within us.

CHAPTER TWO

The Backstory

Through no fault of my parents, this shocking
sequence of events set the stage for the rest of my life.

The recovery meeting where I encountered Gerry wasn't my first. No, what led to that fateful day had started years before. It began when I attended my first recovery meeting at the insistence of my therapist, whom I saw twice a week. I had a Tuesday afternoon private session with her and a Thursday evening group session. My alcoholic tendencies, such as high anxiety, anger, and aggression, came up most often in group sessions, and my therapist would take every opportunity to point them out, urging me to go to a recovery meeting. If not for an attractive young woman in the group who offered to go with me to a meeting, I would have never gone. Perhaps she and the therapist were in cahoots; I don't know. Nevertheless, I am sure they both knew it was the only way to get me to go. It was apparent that I was enslaved to an insatiable need for love and attention from the opposite sex.

I nervously met my female chaperone outside an old church. We walked down the stairs and found two seats in an already packed room. The meeting began, and soon the speaker who sat behind the podium shared his story. He spoke about his first taste of alcohol as a young boy and the feeling of finding what he called a long-lost friend. Yes, a friend: the bottle, which would remain a close companion for a considerable period. He described his adolescence and young adulthood: the parties, the music, the dancing, the girls, and the laughs. It was all good fun and happy times. But it didn't last. And although he tried desperately to hold onto his youth, hanging out with like-minded folks who enjoyed the bar scene with all its glitter, hopes, and dreams of a spectacular future, his life started to sour. Late nights led to hangovers, to calling in sick for work, to "hair of the dog," to lying, to making up excuses, and to trying to stave off the shame by drowning himself in a drink by noon each day. Yes, his talk was a forewarning. He was revealing how addiction inevitably leads to a rock bottom: divorce, heartbreak, joblessness, financial ruin, and lament over the loss of all our hopes of a happy, fruitful, successful life. On top of that, once our standing gets really low and we think we've hit our rock bottom, we can't assume we've reached it, because it can always get worse.

During his story I unexpectedly started to shiver, squeezing my chaperone's hand while holding back tears. I shook, my skin flushed, and I got lightheaded and faint. His story was my story. His pain was my pain. Up until then, I didn't even know what an alcoholic was, much less had ever considered I was one. But there was no question about it; I knew it then and there that I was an alcoholic.

The speaker went on with his story. He spoke of his recovery and his spiritual transformation. He spoke of a sober life, a Higher Power he chose to call God, and of, as he put it, miracles. It was all startling and overwhelming. The meeting ended, and I took a few moments to collect myself. I walked my charitable, compassionate chaperone to the street and flagged down a taxi for her. I thanked her and walked to the nearest subway stop. On my train ride home that night I made a decision to stop drinking. And I've never picked up alcohol again.

You see, the speaker behind the podium at that meeting, this wise gentleman, described, defined, and characterized the alcoholic—and the drug addict, for that matter. He revealed to me that the average alcoholic isn't who you might expect: the wino begging for money, the hardcore drunk sleeping on the street, the destitute person drugged up and dozed off in a dark alleyway. No, many alcoholics and addicts have seemingly functional lives and successful careers. It's the person next door, your neighbor, your kid's schoolteacher, the mail carrier, your cousin, your uncle. He's the affluent Wall Street investment banker who is hooked on internet porn. She's the unhappy housewife who misuses her prescribed sedatives to get through the day. He's the guy who places bet after bet, trying to win back his losses. She's the funny but secretly depressed friend who drinks too much wine at dinner. The thing is, the alcoholic or addict is someone we all know.

Even though I finally put down the drink that day, it was only the beginning of my journey. I continued going to recovery meetings. There was something about being with other alcoholics; we understood each other's plight. But outside of the meetings, life went on. And I soon discovered that without my medicine, alcohol, I was having a tough time of it. My reasons for drinking were becoming apparent. My emotions were slowly and uncontrollably erupting. I was turning into an ugly, angry monster, attacking anyone who annoyed me. And it seemed as if everyone annoyed me. I couldn't bottle up my frustrations and impatience toward people and life without my trusty old friend, booze.

Now, to be clear, the recovery meetings offered more; they suggested a spiritual way of living. But I was an atheist at the time and too smart for my own good. I didn't need help! I was going to figure out sobriety on my own through therapy, self-examination, self-study, and self-help. I didn't need a recovery sponsor or spiritual guide. And I didn't need to go to meetings any longer, for that matter. A few years of meetings was enough. I eventually stopped attending them. For six years I white-knuckled it and lived as a "dry drunk," meaning I was sober but struggling emotionally and psychologically and *acting* like an alcoholic. I was incapable of healthy relationships, whether friendships or romantic ones. Yes, sobriety was exposing the reasons why

I drank in the first place, and these issues were progressively getting worse. Undoubtedly, my drinking problem was a symptom of something deeper.

Nevertheless, I managed to meet a woman and get married—again. My first marriage was short-lived and had ended years earlier, before the thought of sobriety was even a seed in my mind. This new marriage was a loving one. But my wife's biological clock was ticking; we were both older, and it was now or never. So I found myself being a father for the first time, caring for a beautiful, healthy daughter. She was a wonderful, well-behaved infant. All the same, I was slowly losing my sh*t. The world no longer revolved around me. Her existence mirrored back to me my egocentric mindset. This was a difficult transition. Not only that but being responsible for this little soul stirred up such immense anxiety in me that I became frozen with fear and overwhelmed with worry about her well-being and safety.

I was at a point of desperation. A friend suggested a recovery meeting he had been attending. He gave me the address of the Serenity Club. I imagined a basement of a church, but when I arrived, I found myself in front of a run-down, stark-white storefront with turquoise trim that was adjacent to a flower shop and a car wash. The entrance led to a steep flight of stairs. On the second floor, I entered a large antiseptic room where several people were chatting and making tea and coffee, a common sight at recovery meetings. They greeted me, and I took a seat and watched others trickle in. The chairperson arrived and seated himself. He introduced himself as Gerry H.

I continued going to meetings at the Serenity Club for the next couple of weeks, watching Gerry consistently carry the message of recovery with such credence. Still, I had reservations about asking him for help, being that he was a spiritual guy and I was an atheist. But as I said, I was desperate. I was at an impasse. I knew I was broken and unable to help myself. Finally, I conjured up the courage to introduce myself to him. He later claimed I showed him a wallet-size picture of my infant daughter that night, telling him that I didn't believe in God but I saw God in her eyes. I suppose I really was distraught, because I don't recall saying that. We exchanged numbers, and I said good night. Looking back, undoubtedly, my daughter was the primary force that led me to the Serenity Club that night.

I must have looked at Gerry's number a dozen times. Getting a phone number is one thing; making the call is another. As was typical of me, I needed a push. After seeing the state I was in, my therapist (the same one who had sent me to my first recovery meeting six years prior) insisted I call Gerry and ask him for help. I had spoken about Gerry over the weeks, and she knew I was taken by his manner and mindset. So, I called him and asked him for help.

Not that I hadn't sought help before. Long before I stopped drinking, I spent many years in psychotherapy. Through the therapeutic process I discovered numerous reasons I was having difficulties in life, including an early childhood trauma that essentially broke me. When I was three years old, both of my parents had heart attacks within a few months of each other. Neither of them died, but from the eyes of a three-year-old, they did. Taken over by both the physical and emotional toll of their conditions, they were not able to care for me. Fortunately, my grandmother and two older sisters watched over me. Through no fault of my parents, this shocking sequence of events set the stage for the rest of my life. Thankfully they both recovered from their heart attacks, but life for me would never be the same.

Months later, while looking at a science picture book before turning the lights out, I came upon an image of the Earth exploding to bits after a devastating hit from a comet. That fright, to my recollection, initiated the first of many panic attacks to come. My mother had to lie on top of me in bed to stop me from convulsing. At four years old I was already emotionally disabled.

I also suffered from frequent ear infections and fevers that caused me to hallucinate. I have vivid memories of lying in bed, burning up with a high temperature, watching the television set expanding in size, moving toward me as if to swallow me. My mother would have a tough time trying to soothe me.

Life went on—that is, until my first day of school. Outside the doors of the school, I refused to leave my mother and had to be torn from her arms. The teachers dragged me into the school as I violently kicked and screamed. Each day after school, I desired to be home with my mother and my games, hobbies, and favorite TV shows. I'd quietly and happily spend hours alone in my room.

Fortunately, I eventually found a healthy escape—a musical talent. When I turned ten, my father suggested taking drum lessons. I took to it immediately. I would whack the rubber practice pad with my drumsticks for hours and hours. After a year, my parents saw how strong my interest was and bought a drum set for me. I fell in love with it. The practice room was my place of solace.

I excelled as a musician but fell behind in school. In class, my anxiety soared. I couldn't focus. I started compulsively counting numbers in my head. *One, two, three, four. One, two, three. One, two, three, four. One, two, three,* and on and on. Four sets of alternating groups of four and three. Four sets of four. Four sets of three. I counted the tiles on the floor and the tiles on the ceiling. I tapped my hands on the desk—right, right, left, left, four times. And right, left; right, right; left, right; left, left, in sets of four. These were double stroke rolls and single paradiddles. They were among the many drum rudiments that I pedantically practiced. If I flubbed, I had to start over again. I became enslaved to this system of numbers.

I began washing my hands in numerical sets, brushing my teeth four times on each side in sets of four or three, and combing my hair in groups of numbers on the top, sides, and back. If I lost count, I had to begin again. I set the alarm clock on the hour or in increments of five: 7:10, 7:15, 7:20, 7:25, and so on. Never could I set it at odd times like 7:01 or 7:03. As a young adult, I started to double-, triple-, and quadruple-check door locks and stovetop knobs. I remember the unease in my body, which would get worse unless I perfectly performed all my compulsive rituals. A feeling of foreboding would arise, as if something bad would happen if I didn't complete them. It was all-consuming and exhausting. As a consequence, I was often late leaving the house, tardy for school, rushing to make scheduled appointments, and frequently failing to meet my family and friends on time. I never told anyone about my idiosyncrasies. I didn't have a name for it or an understanding of what I was doing, only that I couldn't stop it. I knew something was wrong and that whatever it was, it was surely and swiftly getting worse.

Years later, when I was in my late twenties, I was diagnosed with obsessive-compulsive disorder (OCD), chronic depression, and anxiety disorder. This strange sickness, OCD, that I had kept well-hidden for many years had a name. I was not alone; others suffered from compulsive rituals and obsessive thoughts as well.

The psychiatrist prescribed antidepressants and antianxiety medications. For years I experimented with different dosages and numerous combinations, but nothing helped. What's more, the side effects were severe. Worth noting, though, is that I drank excessively and used drugs recreationally during this time, which, in case it has to be said, didn't give the psychiatric meds a fair shake at helping me.

During this time, I voraciously read self-help books, explored exercise programs, and tried various diets. Still, nothing seemed to do the trick. I had hopeful, short-lived stages of happiness, but they always slipped away. I felt depressed and unhappy. I was on the edge, and my life was turning darker. Anxiety was encapsulating me. I was out of options.

Nothing and no one kept me happy. Discontentment prevailed. Happiness remained out of reach. My search for a better life turned futile. Career success seemed unattainable, and friendships and romances reliably fizzled. Fear had set in, fear that my life would never change, that I would perpetually reside in a prison of depression and anxiety. But now, fortunately, Gerry said he would become my sponsor.

CHAPTER THREE

Self-Help vs. Unself-Help

Many of us who suffer from anxiety, depression, anger issues, or addiction are unable to choose the positive over the negative.

Self-help is the action or process of bettering oneself or overcoming one's problems without the aid of others, especially in the form of trying to cope with one's personal or emotional problems without professional help. Although many people appear to benefit from self-help methods, my view is that their efficacy is limited

Why does self-help seem to work for some people? Likely, it's because they fall into the family of the fortunate few who aren't broken. Meaning, they aren't stricken with debilitating anxiety, alcoholism, or depression. They have the energy to get out of bed bright and early, go to the gym, shower and suit up for work, raise children, continue their education, and entertain on the weekends. They create secure family ties, maintain their religious and family traditions, and cultivate close circles of friends and colleagues. They have active, meaningful social lives, and they establish a strong identity and sense of place in the world. They have the appearance of being able to choose the positive over the negative, happiness over sadness, and forgiveness over holding grudges. Everything works out well for them, or at least well enough. They deal with life's difficulties soundly and have stable support networks to lean on during the more troubling times, such as a divorce, loss, or death. They function in a healthy manner, and self-help provides them with a toolbox that improves their lives. There is seldom a reason to seek professional help, never mind spiritual help.

If only it were that simple for all of us. Unfortunately, it is not. Many of us who suffer from anxiety, depression, anger issues, or addiction are unable to choose the positive over the negative, lack the energy to help others, and, contrary to what many self-help gurus preach, cannot "choose to be happy." These choices are unavailable to us. And all the imparted wisdom from aspiring and well-intentioned people only leaves us uninspired and un-lifted. Motivational quotes like "Believe in yourself," "Hope is the one thing stronger than fear," and "You are stronger than you think" only make us feel worse, less-than, and lacking. This was certainly the case with me. "What's wrong with me? Why can't I just be happy?" I felt weak-willed.

Trauma and perhaps a tender predisposition pulled me down into an early depression. I never knew what it was like to *not* be depressed. I never fell into a depression to know I was in one. My life didn't dramatically change one day, as though I was once productive, social, optimistic, hopeful, and happy and then suddenly found myself to be quite the contrary. I was never optimistic, hopeful, or happy to begin with, so there was no contrast. I had nothing to compare my depression to because I didn't know any different. Depression was all I knew. I always felt alienated, alone, and deeply uneasy, as far back as I can remember. I was like a camera eye viewing the world from a distance, separate from the world and other people, on the outside looking in, uncomfortable in my skin. My life was always cloudy and skewed. And over the years it grew darker.

I adopted a negative view of the world, turning cynical, pessimistic, and sarcastic. I developed a doom-and-gloom attitude. As I saw it, happiness was a foolish, unrealistic notion that only blissfully light-hearted people feigned. They weren't really happy; they were just good fakers possessing phony smiles. Yes, I had it all figured out. I was too smart for my own good (at least that's what I thought). I knew that happiness didn't exist. And most people were unwilling to admit to it. They wouldn't dare consider it. They didn't have the nerve to acknowledge a harsh reality that was too brutal to accept.

Over time, I turned nihilistic. And I explored this state of being. I dwelled on suicidal scenarios and stepped into sexcapades such as sadomasochism (S&M) and bondage. On top of that, I experimented with harder drugs—cocaine, heroin, and morphine—and I became a heavy drinker. Life was at least tolerable when I was intoxicated and high—although I could never maintain that state. Indeed, looking back, my depression had defeated me. Life had no meaning. It was a cruel and painful cosmic farce.

No matter what I did to try to improve myself, I perceived myself as a failure and a loser, even though my family and friends would tell me otherwise: "We are so proud of you." "You're a talented and gifted man." Their support was appreciated, but I never believed them. Essentially, self-help methods didn't work for me because my *self* was broken. I needed outside help, both professionally and spiritually. And this is especially important when it comes to conditions such as anxiety, depression, alcoholism, and addiction. Plainly, we cannot just *be* happy. We can't just *be* content and joyful. We can't just pretend to possess purpose and meaning, a positive attitude, and a general sense of well-being. If it were that simple, we would all be happy.

But sometimes the self is stubborn. Our ego thinks it's going to figure it all out. It eggs us on, coerces us, and convinces us that things will be different this time around. "I'm going to wake up tomorrow and choose to be happy." So we endlessly amass arsenals of self-help offerings that promise to service us in our endeavor. We post affirmations on our fridge, memorize inspirational quotes, and tell ourselves that we deserve all the things we wish for in life. Indeed, adages like "Don't sweat the small stuff" and "Stop and smell the roses" may give us a moment of pause and hope, but once the moment passes, we find ourselves shouting at our partner for leaving the front door unlocked.

16

Nothing seems to do the trick; still, we carry on seeking aphorisms, sharing them on social media. "Hey guys, 'Don't worry; be happy; life is too short.'" Our ego resists and blinds us from seeing that we cannot help ourselves. Indian thinker and spiritual teacher Osho explains,

> *All efforts to improve yourself are bound to fail because the one who is making the effort is the problem: the ego. The ego is constantly making efforts to improve: have more money, have a bigger house, have a bigger car, have a more beautiful woman, or a husband, have this, have that. That is ego. ... But then the ego plays another game too: It says, "Become more peaceful, become more loving, ... be like a buddha." This again is the same game in another direction. The same ego that was trying to decorate itself with outer things now wants to try and decorate itself with inner things.[2]*

The self-help guru will

> *tell you that the best answer is to think positive thoughts, to be peaceful, ... by repeating affirmations, such as "All is light," "All is God," "All is good," or whatever it may be. But unfortunately it doesn't always work because you have a nagging suspicion in the back of your mind that you're simply hypnotizing yourself and whistling in the dark.[3]*

Yes, in their desire to inspire, the enthusiastic guru assures us, "You are not broken; you don't need to be fixed; you were born a sensitive person. If you feel alone and afraid, it's because you haven't found your tribe yet. If you're easily hurt, it's your place in life; you're an empath." This message may be one of good will, but it closes the door to transformation that will alleviate our suffering. In effect, it's saying, "You are already perfect; the problem is everyone else and the world around you."

On the other hand, the spiritual work, or what we can call the unself work, encourages us to acknowledge and accept our current condition, but it does not suggest we settle for it and justify it. On the contrary, the spiritual work asks us to objectively and honestly look at ourselves. It asks us to get humble. It requires us to admit that we are broken and flawed. And although it teaches us that it's okay to be broken because it is human, it guides us and empowers us to rewrite our story. When we begin to embrace rather than deny our imperfections, we open up to grace and all possibilities. At the same time, we cannot do it alone. We need help. And here lies the difference between self-help and the spiritual work: Self-help is asking the self to help the self, while the spiritual work draws from a Power greater than ourselves. The spiritual work asks us, the self, to surrender to something bigger than the self. Fundamentally, it asks us to *unself*.

The spiritual work is not a mental process—it's a way of living: "The spiritual life is not a theory. We have to live it."[4] And when we do, we subsequently tap into another level of thinking, an inner strength, a deeper wisdom, and a Power greater than our *self*. This is the distinction between self-help and the spiritual work.

As we unself, our focus shifts. We learn to let go of the notion that something on the outside is going to generate happiness, and the causes of our suffering come to light. When we get acquainted with the causes and concentrate on how we can suffer less, we find connection and happiness within us. We get out of our own way, and a door opens up to something greater—that is to say, something bigger than our *self*, something outside our *self*: the transcendence of self.

CHAPTER FOUR

The Inside Work: Taking Pen to Paper

It struck me hard. I was shocked.
I had had no idea what harm I had done.

Becoming a parent turned out to be the perfect remedy for an egocentric person like myself. My wants and needs had to take a back seat. This was difficult but good for me. At the time, my wife and I were both working, making a decent buck. We had a good health insurance plan, we were pursuing our dreams and goals, and we were having a healthy sex life. In spite of that, about six months after my daughter's birth something terribly disturbing happened.

Although our daughter was perfectly healthy and well-tempered, my concern about her well-being began to grow. I quickly became overwhelmed with fear and worry. I didn't know how to handle being a parent, and my apprehension over her health and safety increased. I began to have strong suicidal thoughts again. And for the first time in my life, I started having homicidal thoughts. It scared the hell out of me. I fell into a state of despair and turned deathly afraid. Although I knew I could never harm my family, the thoughts shook me to the core.

This was when my therapist insisted I call Gerry H. After telling her about my distressing thoughts, she gave me an ultimatum: "Either you call up Gerry right now and arrange to meet with him tonight, or I am checking you into a psychiatric hospital." Again, my therapist sent me in the right direction; I called Gerry up and met with him that night.

I didn't have to make a decision, take a leap of faith, or step out of my comfort zone—I had no choice in the matter; my pain was too great. After years of therapy, a long phase of taking prescription pharmaceuticals, six years of abstinence from drugs and alcohol, various exercise and nutrition programs, and self-help courses, I had reached a dead end. I had no other alternatives available to me. There may have been forces at work, or perhaps it was simply the will to survive, but something led me to Gerry.

"No coincidences. God's a master chess player," Gerry used to say. True or not, the stage was set. He graciously and generously offered to work with me. I didn't believe the recovery program would help me, but I trusted Gerry, which was odd—because I didn't trust anyone. This was my introduction to doing the unself work.

Still, I was resistant. I fought Gerry tooth and nail, rebelling against his suggestions and instructions. I argued with him frequently, but he tolerated me. I think it was because he understood me. He knew what it was like. He had once been like me. And although I wanted to give up many times, he never gave up on me. I would often tell him he was wasting his time, that I was beyond hope. But he never backed down. He was unyielding. I see now that I needed tough love, and Gerry was the right guy for the job. He was a pit bull but a compassionate one.

Gerry had many years of experience helping others. He also had what we all wanted: sobriety and peace of mind. He was a beacon, a burning torch, and we all knew it. His unbounded gratitude was palpable. Of all his qualities, what was most foreign to me was his strong yearning to help fellow sufferers. He devoted his life to being of service to others. All else was secondary. He saw it as doing God's work. It was his covenant with God. He expressed to me that he received "the Power and the grace" by carrying the message of recovery and serving God and others: "Power" meaning a Higher Power, a Power greater than ourselves, and "grace" meaning (in the Christian sense)

God's benevolence toward the unworthy. Yes, he believed this deep down in his soul.

As for me, God was a hard sell. I didn't believe in Him. I'd lost my faith long ago. Religion and spirituality were of no interest to me. I had little trust, hope, or promise in a spiritual solution to my problems. I was skeptical, to say the least. But I was suffering. And so I found myself taking on a far-fetched proposition. According to Alcoholics Anonymous (AA) literature, "Someone who knew what he was talking about once remarked that pain was the touchstone of all spiritual progress."[5] These words certainly applied to me. I didn't voluntarily choose to walk the spiritual path; it was out of pure pain, desperation, and despair.

When it came to God, Gerry suggested I stay open and willing, that through the recovery work, I would find a God of my understanding. Until then, Gerry urged me to "fake it till you make it." He got me on my knees—which at that critical point in my life didn't take much effort. He worked with me every day. To be sure, I was difficult. Not on the grounds that I was unwilling to do the work but because I made him work hard. Many of his standard suggestions and instructions weren't enough for me. I needed more. I made him dig deeper to find ways to prove to me that this spiritual way of living was legitimate. He had the patience of a saint, answered my queries, and put up with most of my unreasonable requests. This was around the time I took a broader interest in Buddhism and Yoga. The ideas and teachings of these practices turned out to be a well-needed adjunct to the recovery work.

Why We Suffer

The Buddha came upon a profound understanding while meditating under a bodhi tree. The Four Noble Truths were his first teachings revealing this understanding.

21

The First Truth—*all life is suffering*—exhibits the reality of life: aging, sickness, separation, unceasing desire, disappointment, and death. This reality causes an undercurrent of fear and anxiety.

The Second Truth reveals that *suffering is caused by craving*. "I want that job." "You can't leave me; you're my wife till death do us part." "I want my father back; he didn't deserve to die." "I don't want to grow old." We crave satisfaction, stability, and security. We struggle with what Buddhists call *impermanence*.

Nothing seems to satisfy us. People don't live up to our expectations; our salary isn't satisfactory; we thirst for a thinner body, a better job, and a bigger home; we are married to someone yet longing to be with someone else. This inability to enjoy what we already have causes suffering and steals our serenity.

We expend exorbitant amounts of energy trying to escape our discontent, and we do so by way of externals. We change our environment, go from one job to another, move from one part of the country to another; yet nothing cuts us loose from the cravings and restlessness. Although initially we might find relief, it is always short-lived. This is because nothing on the outside is going to fix things. We strive to make more money in the hopes of harnessing happiness. We acquire much more than we need, working long hours and long workweeks to afford all the new gadgets and the trendiest new lines of clothing. We fall victim to consumerism propaganda. We buy into the promise that status goods, such as owning the highest priced car, will bring us joy. We believe that luxury travel and services such as flying first class to the most exotic locations, staying in five-star hotels, and dining in upscale restaurants will bring us happiness. Indeed, the sensual world is lovely, but it's not the path to happiness. We need something more. Alone, sensuality is just another form of escapism. Sure, bathing and luxuriating in the beauty of the French Alps may lift us up, but it will not aid us in dealing with a sudden death of a loved one or help us embrace our mortality. The problem is that we want something other than reality.

The Third Truth: *Craving can be overcome* once we stop struggling and abandon expectations and wants.

The Fourth Truth states that *the way to overcome craving is the path of mindfulness and awareness*, essentially spiritual work that addresses the inner life. The idea here is that if we live in accordance with these principles (known as the Eightfold Path), we can free ourselves from craving and suffering.

Getting Out of Our Own Way

Along those same lines, Gerry pressed me to abandon self-analysis. "Stop analyzing everything. That's your problem; you analyze too much. Stop, let it go, and trust God." He wanted me to stop trying to figure things out. This was difficult for me at first. I wanted to understand everything and make sense of my problems. But Gerry stood firm. When I was put off by someone or something, he would assert, "Don't analyze it; just get rid of it." For an analytical guy like me this seemed illogical. My preference was to pick things apart, to find meaning for everything.

I remember Gerry asserting, "If you step in dog poop, get something to wipe it off your shoe and go about your day. Carl, your problem is that you want to look at it, smell it, study it, and put it in a baggie to analyze later. It's poop, Carl. It's negative; get rid of it." But I was hardheaded and too ego-driven to give up on solving my own problems. I was not going to unself easily. And so, as it turned out, I had to get emotionally beaten up a few more times before I threw in the towel.

Gerry often said that I was the problem and I needed to get out of my own way and surrender to God, remarking that I was too smart

23

for my own good. This made no sense to me at the time, but I came to realize that my way was not working for me. Clergy and author Eugene Peterson said it well: "You're not trying to figure things out; you're trying to enter into what's there."[6]

Gerry maintained that my thinking was upside down and twisted. He instructed me to think, say, and do the opposite of what I wanted. This was how to practice unselfing, how to practice the spiritual work. He'd say, "Keep it simple. If it's negative, get rid of it." If my thoughts were judgmental toward someone, I was to let go of them. If my urge was to be curt, I had to force myself to be friendly. If I wanted to lash out at someone, I was to refrain from the unkind word. Gerry knew that "The thought manifests as the word, the word manifests as the deed, the deed develops into habit, and habit hardens into character," as the saying goes. So, I followed his instructions.

Gerry had me take pen to paper. In fact, he pushed me because he knew I would procrastinate since I hated doing written assignments, especially when it came to self-improvement-like methods. I was never a good student. Besides that, I couldn't see how writing down my fears, resentments, and wrongs could help me. More than that, being an atheist, the God part of the process didn't resonate with me.

He had me list the people who I was angry with and had resentments toward. He told me to write down the reasons I was angry and resentful. Then he asked me to look at where I was mistaken, selfish, dishonest, and wrong. When I was done, he directed me to list my fears, the reasons I had them, how was I supporting them, and how I could handle them better. Afterward, I was to write down who I had hurt in my life, specifically in the realm of romantic and sexual relations. Was I dishonest, unfaithful? Did I evoke feelings of discomfort, doubt, and distrust? How could I have been a better person and partner?

It slowly became apparent that a clearing was being made. A new perspective of the world, previously obscured, grew visible to me. I saw aspects of myself that I didn't want to see, not to mention examine.

Taking pen to paper uncovered a reality outside my egocentric world, breaking down the walls of denial and forcing me to get honest. It was a shocking process of discovery. The role I played in what until now had seemed like a one-sided and clear-cut case of they-were-wrong-I-was-right was revealed to me as the contrary. I had played a major part in all my suffering, and now Gerry was asking me to hold myself accountable. I had to admit my wrongs to myself, Gerry, and God.

Next, we looked at my character flaws. Our flaws are a part of us, integrated into our psyche. They mature into an integral working part of our mind. Most of us are unaware of them. Yet we nurture them and refine them every day, sometimes knowingly, more often not. They become our identity: the cynic, the sarcastic one, the life of the party, the tough guy, the one who can hold his liquor, the depressive, or whatever. For better or for worse, some of us wear our labels proudly and they become us. "I'm a hotheaded person. It's just the way I am." It takes great effort to rid ourselves of our flaws. They take on a life of their own, and they don't die easy.

Likely our shortcomings have more of an impact on our lives than we are willing to admit. In fact, I am convinced that they are among the many causes of our suffering. It may be difficult to consider that one or two character flaws in a person could undermine all their good traits, but think about it: A bad temper, a cynical outlook, or a sarcastic attitude can easily overshadow and corrode a person's good qualities. They might be talented, intelligent, educated, and generous yet unpleasant and difficult to be around. Just a few flaws can inhibit someone from being more successful in life. They can foil a potential career goal and destroy a loving and trusting marriage beyond repair.

We might think, *Sure, I'm not perfect, but these traits are me; they're my personality. Without them, who would I be?* Such was the case with me. I was the tortured artist. For certain, I was the cynical guy with a cigarette dangling between my fingers, a whiskey habitually in my hand, brooding, sarcastic, and disaffected, repeatedly rambling on about suicide and death. The people in my life glamorized and romanticized my persona. "Yeah, Carl's the troubled, tormented artist. He's a dark dude. One of those gifted depressives." And I found myself having to live up to this image, even though I would have traded my troubles for happiness in a heartbeat. But I was stuck. And more than that, what would become of me without this identity? These are the fears that prevent us from exerting ourselves to the extent needed. After all, as Step Six of the Twelve Steps of AA says, "How many of us have this degree of readiness? ... Even then the best of us will discover to our dismay that there is always a sticking point, a point at which we say, 'No, I can't give this up yet.'"[7]

In Gerry's presence, I admitted to him and God my powerlessness. I knew I couldn't proceed relying solely on self-will. And although I was still struggling with finding a Higher Power, I had to humble myself and surrender my will to something beyond myself. Whether that was God, the cosmos, the universe, or the greater good, I had to dig up the willingness to permit this Power to remove my shortcomings.

In his book *Cutting Through Spiritual Materialism*, Tibetan Buddhist monk Chögyam Trungpa writes,

> *We must really surrender, give something, give something up in a very painful way. ... The problem is that we tend to seek an easy and painless answer. But this kind of solution does not apply to the spiritual path, which many of us should not have begun at all. Once we commit ourselves to the spiritual path, it is very painful and we are in for it.*[8]

But there was no turning back now. The spiritual work started to reveal my flaws. It was painful to see and to admit what a sarcastic guy I was and how it was hurting others. Moreover, I was starting to see how my sarcasm was not only an outlet for my anger and discontent, it was fueling them. I followed Gerry's instructions, pausing, refraining, and letting go of the urge to make the sarcastic remark. Gerry knew how difficult this path was, which was why he used to tell me quite often, "Baby steps, Carl; take baby steps." It took some time, but change came. My sarcasm slowly slipped away.

CHAPTER FIVE

Beyond Scientific Explanation

If the anthropomorphized white-bearded, male,
patriarchal God who pulls all the strings is causing
you anguish, perhaps it's time to reevaluate.

Early in my sobriety, before meeting Gerry, I heard a story at a recovery meeting that struck me deep in the gut. This gentleman told us he had shot and killed a taxi driver point blank for no reason other than for the hell of it. He served many years in prison for his crime. While behind bars, he explained how one day he fell to his knees and had what one might call a white-light experience. It was a spiritual awakening. In the blink of an eye, he changed from a cold-blooded killer to this Buddha-like presence who sat there before us all. His presence and aura were nothing short of holy.

While walking home from the meeting, I couldn't hold back the tears. His story was extraordinary, a psychic transformation that seemed beyond scientific explanation. It threatened my methods of recovery. Twenty years of psychotherapy couldn't change a man from a killer to a giver; only something greater and bigger could do that, and do it in a moment's time. When I got home, I collapsed on the floor. I wept uncontrollably. I convulsed. I dry-heaved. This went on until I passed out.

When I came to, I was wiped out and weak. But my skepticism and stubbornness slowly slipped back. I didn't want to go back to believing in God. As an atheist, I had freed myself, for the most part, of those debilitating feelings of guilt and shame I had once lived with. Likewise, believing in the supernatural and living in a magical world had never worked for me. It only led to disappointment after disappointment. Life had never gone as I had wished. I had tried to do the right thing in the hopes that God would reward me with all I prayed for, but I was let down again and again. What's more, I didn't understand why God would take the good people and let the bad ones live. I found it disheartening that He would let terrible things happen to innocent people. Life seemed unfair, and God was unjust, judgmental, and punishing. Without question, the God who my Western roots had planted in me had rotted.

It was a slow, arduous process that took many years, but I had cleaned the slate, as it were, and become an atheist. Still, that wasn't enough. Over and above, for the first few years as an atheist, I spent a great deal of energy trying to disprove the existence of God. No doubt I was difficult to be around. I was the death of many parties. Over time, I simmered down. I settled into a more comfortable, calm place. I stopped being an angry anti-Christian and turned more peaceful. Largely, I was able to live and let live.

It was less painful being an atheist. I freed myself from the punishing, judgmental, authoritative Father I had been taught to believe in. I was happier, though, at the start it was dismal. I had to sit in the nothingness. I had to live each day without a sense of celestial meaning, no afterlife, no cosmic justice—just death, nothing more. And so, I had to find meaning. Without God, I turned to love. Principles such as honesty, justice, and integrity became vitally important. I turned to educating myself by attending college and studying subjects such as cultural anthropology, comparative religion, and Greek theater. I dug more deeply into the sciences: philosophy, psychology, and pharmacology. Learning was eye-opening. Yet I remained angry, resentful, unforgiving, and depressed. There was still something missing.

It was only years later, after getting sober; after working with Gerry; after taking pen to paper; after doing the spiritual work; after helping others in recovery; after diving more deeply into Yoga, Buddhism, Taoism, and the neurosciences; and after connecting with a Power greater than myself that my life fundamentally changed. Religion, spirituality, the sciences, and a God of my understanding suddenly coexisted, and the spiritual realm and the scientific world paralleled one another.

God

This three-letter word has arguably provoked more thought, invoked more investigation, stirred up more debate, and conjured up more emotions than any other word. It carries with it enormous weight, depth, and meaning. The notion of God is a complex one. It can be said that God is undefinable and cannot be fully understood. Yet we tirelessly try to explain, interpret, define, and characterize God, ad nauseam. We doubt, question, and reject God. We distressingly try to comprehend God. We try to prove and disprove God's existence.

Religious and spiritual leaders from various traditions and modern gurus alike have conceptualized God in many different ways, calling Him by innumerable names, such as Creator, Divine One, Source, Higher Power, Infinite Consciousness, a Power greater than ourselves, the Way, *what is*, and the Eternal Now. Countless people have attempted to describe the indescribable, explain the inexplicable, define the undefinable, and prove the unprovable. Yet, and still, God remains an ineffable mystery.

Wilfred Cantwell Smith points out that the concept of religion was a later development in history, thought to have originated about 2,500 years ago.[9] Smith distinguishes between "religion" and "the religions." He defines religion as "cumulative tradition," essentially "anything that can be and is transmitted from one person, one generation, to another, and that an historian can observe,"[10] including "temples, scriptures, theological systems, dance patterns, legal and other social institutions, conventions, moral codes, myths, and so on."[11] "The religions," on the other hand, he describes as "personal faith": in effect, "an inner religious experience or involvement of a particular person; the impingement on him of the transcendent."[12] In *Religious Worlds*, William E. Paden echoes Smith: "Religiousness means engaging the sacred."[13]

Speaking of the sacred, the Eastern religions, which were developed long before the Western religions and Islam, focused mainly on rituals, sacrifices, and transcendence. It was only since the creation of the Western and Islamic institutions that the primary focus shifted, leaning more on the cumulative traditions (dogma and moral codes) and less on religiousness (the personal/inner experience of the sacred). The British and American Buddhist, Taoist, and Hindu philosopher Alan Watts further explains,

> *Religions of Asia ... are interested in changing states of human consciousness. Whereas institutional Western religions—Christianity, Judaism, and even Islam—are relatively less interested in this matter. Western religions are more concerned with behavior, doctrine, and belief than with any transformation of the way in which we are aware of ourselves and of the world.[14]*

I came upon the Eastern religions later in life. Like an earthquake, they shattered my systems of beliefs and shifted my entire perspective. Everything I knew and had learned up until then was turned upside down and inside out. My view of life, death, and the world changed completely. For whatever reason, the church, and its teachings and good intent, did not aid me or comfort me. The doctrines, beliefs, and truths, as I later realized, separated me from the inner experience, making the sacred less personal.

For many in the West, God conjures up unfavorable feelings of guilt and shame. Many reject God, declaring Him unjust. "If God is all-powerful and compassionate, why does He let pure and innocent children die?" Others feel as though God dealt them a bad hand. Nothing goes their way. They pray yet end up empty-handed and disappointed. An innumerable number of God-fearing followers are raised with an angry, judgmental, and punishing God: "The LORD is a jealous and avenging God; the LORD takes vengeance and is filled with wrath. The LORD takes vengeance on his foes and vents his wrath against his enemies."[15] And although this same authoritative God "is love"[16] and "merciful and gracious,"[17] many focus on the wrathful God, who although He is "slow to anger,"[18] righteously judges and punishes sinners, of which we all are: "for all have sinned and fall short of the glory of God."[19]

In their book *How God Changes Your Brain: Breakthrough Findings from a Leading Neuroscientist*, the authors take a closer look at these paradoxes and their effects.

Are there any drawbacks to religious involvement? Yes, but it mostly involves issues concerning anger and fear. ... If you see God as a punishing figure, or have negative attitudes toward the clergy or other church members, you will be inclined toward poorer health and depression. And if you find yourself in conflict with your religious feelings or beliefs, your health can deteriorate and your risk of dying will increase. So by all means, pick a religious system or spiritual practice that makes you feel good about yourself and others.[20]

Questioning our religion and God can be difficult, if not impossible for some. It usually takes an earth-shattering event to shake us up enough to consider such a task. Be that as it may, if the anthropomorphized white-bearded, male, patriarchal God who pulls all the strings is causing you anguish, perhaps it's time to reevaluate. If the God you bargain and negotiate with causes you grief, maybe you should reconsider your relationship with God. If you are living an unfulfilled life, it may be time to rebuild your spiritual life.

The Laws of Nature

Religion and science sometimes seem at odds with one another. There is a skepticism about spirituality in the scientific community and a pushback on some scientific concepts from religious groups and scholars.

In defense of modern science, many questions have been answered about the universe that seem to override the ancient ideas of religion. Science has discovered certain cosmic laws, and these laws have deepened our understanding of the cosmos and changed our view of the world. The father of physics, Sir Isaac Newton, postulated that everything followed fundamental physical laws, as did Albert Einstein years later. They both believed, as some of today's quantum physicists strongly suggest,[21] that a designer or creator put these laws into place, certainly leaving an opening for a religious rebuttal.

Conversely, evolutionary biologist and author Richard Dawkins speculates that

> for early humanity, what was mysterious and unexplained was so vast that only an equally vast, higher being, an alpha male in the sky, could fill that gap. ... In past centuries, humanity had no choice but to resort to a supernatural hypothesis. Among the many creation myths around the world, the book of Genesis imagined a designer god.[22]

All the same, these are theories and hence leave room for argument and debate.

That said, there are fundamental laws that exist that are not based on theory. In fact, they are undeniable and inarguable. These laws, one could say, are spiritual in nature. And they are at the heart of what drives us to create, cohabitate, procreate, and explore the world and the stars. We seldom acknowledge them, if at all, though they shape everything we do:

I am of the nature to grow old. There is no way to escape growing old.

I am of the nature to have ill health. There is no way to escape ill health.

I am of the nature to die. There is no way to escape death.

All that is dear to me and everyone I love are of the nature to change. There is no way to escape being separated from them.

My actions are my only true belongings. I cannot escape the consequences of my actions. My actions are the ground upon which I stand.

These laws or, as I call them, the Laws of Nature, are the Five Remembrances.[23] They were presented by the Buddha. It takes little examination or reflection to realize that they are undebatable and indisputable truths: we age, we get ill, we die, people change and leave us, and our choices have consequences. They are spiritual in that they exist outside the intellectual and material realms. Beyond that, they have a psychological and emotional component to them. They touch on the human condition and the human spirit. In this sense, they can be called spiritual laws. Yet they are not faith-based, nor are they evidence-based (on the order of science, as in they can be measured and tested in the same manner as formulaic laws like E=mc²). No, these laws are incorporeal.

The Buddha recommends we meditate on the Five Remembrances every day, which may urge you to ask, "Why on earth would one want to think about, never mind meditate on, illness, death, and loss? These are the very things we ward off at length and desperately don't want to look at or think about!" You're right in that we incorporate a great amount of ingenuity avoiding these formidable thoughts. We urgently try to outsmart them, run from them, and push them away—sometimes consciously but more often unconsciously. So then, why would the Buddha offer up such a seemingly morbid task? Well, the short answer is that our attempts at ignoring them sustains them and the subsequent feelings of unease, restlessness, and dread. As much as we try to dodge them, outwit them, deny them, and cover them up, on some level, they will negatively affect us until we pay attention to them.

But what are we trying to escape, exactly? Well, the obvious answer would be aging, sickness, death, loss, and the consequences of our choices. Basically, impermanence and the fear and unease it produces. Essentially, we are trying to escape reality by running away from the laws of nature, laws that boast the same concepts found in many Western and Eastern religious and spiritual writings in respect to God.

From this perspective, science tells us that the universe is made up of energy and that energy cannot be created or destroyed. It is also said that God was not created and cannot be destroyed. This can also be said about the Five Remembrances. With that, couldn't we surmise that energy, the Five Remembrances, and God are one and the same? So then, are we trying to evade God?

Even further, provided we integrate the physicist's perspective that the universe follows fundamental physical laws and also assume that a designer put these laws into place, couldn't we conceivably hypothesize that the designer is the design? Which is to say, that God, the laws, and the design are one? In other words, God is not necessarily the designer but the design itself.

Another way to view these laws is by means of metaphysics, which is a branch of philosophy that dates as far back as ancient Greece. It is the study of the nature of reality beyond the physical—what is outside the material world and objective experience—the fundamental nature of *being* and the universe. In Aristotelian terms, metaphysics refers to *things that do not change.* In Chinese philosophy, this concept is called the Tao. Legend has it that Lao Tzu, considered the father of Taoism, wrote the text *Tao Te Ching* in the fourth century BC. It has been translated as "The Book of the Way."[24] And the Tao, which means "the way or path," "is beyond form ... beyond sound ... intangible ... indefinable and beyond description."[25]

The spiritual practice of Taoism, as well as Buddhism and the Hindu philosophy Advaita, are called nonduality traditions. The concept of nondualism or nonduality means "not two." We are one, not separate, and we cannot be separated from this oneness. It is everything, but it is nothing. It is *what is* and *what is not.* It cannot be defined or understood. At the same time, all is complete, perfect, as it is, as it should be, and it cannot be changed. We cannot be outside it looking in or inside it looking out. It is omnipresent. Again, not unlike God.

If the universe is made up of energy, then this would mean that we are made up of energy, that "We are made of star stuff."[26] And so, if energy, the Five Remembrances, and a God of our understanding are one, then we must be as well. In which case, we can say that we are God manifested; "We're in the universe and the universe is in us."[27] That being the case, are we then trying to escape ourselves? Are we trying to escape life itself?

I am certainly not suggesting that we all want to die. These urges to escape the laws work on an unconscious level. What I *am* proposing, though, is that we are trying to transcend life. From a psychological standpoint, we are yearning to integrate our conscious and unconscious mind. Which is to say, we are trying to transcend suffering. In effect, we are longing for oneness with God. Only we don't know it. And in view of not *knowing*, we search for things outside ourselves that give us that feeling of transcendence. Again, Watts:

> *It should be obvious that the human being "goes with" the rest of the universe, even though we say in popular speech, "I came into this world." Now, it is not true that you came into this world, you came out of it in the same way as a flower comes out of a plant or a fruit comes out of a tree. And as an apple tree apples, the solar system in which we live … peoples. And therefore, people are an expression of its energy and of its nature.*[28]

This idea of energy expressing itself is like the concept found in some religions that contends that human beings are created in the likeness of God. We only have to look at the self-replicating molecule, the beginning of life as we know it; couldn't this be God expressing Himself in all living things?

Whether or not these viewpoints resonate with us, and regardless of whether we believe in a God of our understanding or not, we are all still subject to the laws of nature. Whatever name we choose for them, be it the Five Remembrances, the laws of nature, cosmic law, universal truths, or God, what matters is our relationship to them. With that said, what I discovered is this: Accepting and surrendering to these laws and what we are powerless over—aging, sickness, death, loss, and the consequences of our actions—enables us to transcend fear and, hence, suffer less. And, as such, we become one and in harmony with these laws, tapping into a power, wisdom, and strength inside us and beyond us. That is the spiritual work, the work of unselfing.

CHAPTER SIX

Being Spiritual

I thought that if I worked diligently toward achieving my goals and did the "right thing" that God would save me from my suffering.

When I was presented with the truth of it in the rooms of recovery—that alcoholism is a spiritual malady that can only be overcome by being spiritual—I found myself at a crossroads. I was admittedly an alcoholic, but I did not want to live a religious or spiritual life, nor did I believe it would make a difference. There had to be another way.

As it turned out, I didn't even know what being spiritual meant. Sure, plenty of us have preconceived notions: for example, that you must "sell your possessions and give to the poor."[29] I thought I would have to be a missionary or live like a monk and give up all my worldly pleasures. Living a spiritual life seemed unrealistic and far-fetched, so I rejected the notion. That is, until a feeling of hopelessness and despair overwhelmed me and my suffering became too much to bear, which was when and why I started the spiritual work with Gerry.

Over time, I learned that being spiritual means unselfing, and this takes hard work. For me it entailed a daily practice of filtering all my thoughts, words, and actions. I had to slowly let go of the old self to allow the new one to be born. Whatever that new self might turn out to be, I had to trust my Higher Power, be open and patient, and let this new life reveal itself to me.

This spiritual model for living was unlike anything I observed as a youth. Most churchgoers I knew reserved their time with God and their best behavior for Sundays. They'd smile, shake hands, serve coffee and cake after the service, and share stories about their faith. Then they would go about their week as they always did, displaying impatience toward their work colleagues, getting angry with their children, and drinking a bit too much in the evenings.

Buddhist author and meditation teacher Sharon Salzberg recounts a story that took place back in the early 1970s. While working with others for a few years as a meditation teacher, she and her group sent for one of their teachers in India to see the progress they had made in America. The teacher's name was Manindra. When he arrived, Salzberg expressed to him her excitement about how some people were beginning to take an interest in meditation. "Isn't it wonderful?" she asked.

And he said, "Oh, it is wonderful, and there's just this one thing," he said. "Some of these people in the West remind me of people sitting in a rowboat, and with great sincerity and earnestness they're rowing and rowing and rowing, but they refuse to untie the boat from the dock." He said, "Sometimes I think people are mostly interested in these great, transcendent experiences and altered states of consciousness, but they're not all that interested in how they speak to their neighbor or how they are with their children."[30]

Long before working with Gerry, I never thought of spirituality as a way of living, as something I'd have to work at or practice. I believed there would come a day when everything would just click and it would all make sense; I'd wake up believing in God and go on my merry way. I didn't know that inner peace and happiness take hard work, that I'd have to surrender to a Higher Power, accept what is, meditate, pray, reflect on my fear and anger, make amends, and help others on a daily basis. I didn't know it requires an unselfish and self-sacrificing lifestyle change.

Back when I was deep in my depression, I didn't believe that helping others could drag me out of despair, just as I didn't believe that a spiritual recovery program could help me. I mean, how could it help me to write down my resentments and make amends to the people I'd wronged (see Chapters 14 and 13)? Likewise, I didn't believe that a physical activity like yoga could help cure me of my depression (see Chapter 10). And I didn't believe that my heavy drinking and drugging had anything to do with my depression and unhappiness. But in every case, I was wrong, dead wrong.

In my egocentric world, I thought that if I worked diligently toward achieving my goals and did the "right thing" that God would save me from my suffering. I believed He would bestow upon me the gracious gifts of a good life, that everything would fall into place, that all my hopes and dreams would come true, that I would find a soulmate; have a successful career; make a great deal of money; be praised by my peers; become a patient, peaceful person; and live a comfortable life. But again, I was wrong.

What Is Surrender?

"Me, surrender? Never! Giving up is not part of my vocabulary." The idea of surrender is unalluring, repellent, and outright repugnant to many of us. Generally viewed as resignation, surrendering is considered emblematic of a weak-willed, defeated person. "Oh, I give up; I can't take it anymore; I haven't the strength or will to go on." We have a strong aversion to surrendering, and this disinclination is understandable, natural, and even hardwired. We want agency, autonomy, independence, and freedom. We want to fight for what we believe in, no matter the cost. The reason for our resistance is apparent. Or so it seems.

Looking further, it becomes clear that self-will, ego, and fear accompany our dislike of the idea of surrendering. We want to feel in control of our lives and environment; we want to feel powerful. I believe our reluctance toward the idea of surrendering is that we think of surrender as submission. After all, surrender *is* defined as such:

To yield to the power, control or of possession of another upon compulsion or demand.

To give up completely or agree to forgo especially in favor of another.

To give (oneself) up into the power of another especially as a prisoner.

To give (oneself) over to something (as an influence).[31]

Waving a white flag, as if we lost the battle, and yielding to the power of another is unappealing and undesirable. But when we look at surrender from a spiritual point of view, it takes on an entirely different meaning. In the spiritual context, surrendering is not the same as submitting. In fact, it is the polar opposite. When we submit, there is fear, anxiety, and disempowerment. When we surrender within the framework of spirituality, there is joy, calm, and empowerment. In fact, surrender is the most important aspect of the unself work.

To illustrate surrender, imagine a man jumping into the strong current of an ocean, putting his life at risk to save another from drowning. There isn't a *thinking* process; there is just an *action*. He acts quickly without thinking, even in the bosom of fear. This is an act of surrender. This type of determination, when observed, touches us right at our core. It penetrates our hearts. It is a heroic act that has little to do with machismo, ego, pride, or reward. There is something more profound at play, something spiritual, an interconnectedness between all living beings, a shining display of the human spirit. Whether we witness or participate in such acts of fortitude, we are transported out of self. And what occurs, beyond our conscious awareness, is a oneness with everything.

On the other hand, one doesn't have to perform heroic acts to feel interconnected. Just look lovingly into your child's eyes, pause to take a deep breath while walking in nature, or bow and pray to God, and

> *you feel completely* with *this universe. You feel profoundly rooted in it and connected with it. You feel, in other words, that the whole energy which expresses itself in the galaxies is intimate. It is not something to which you are a stranger, but it is that with which you (whatever that is) are intimately bound up.*[32]

Acknowledging our oneness is a form of surrender that reveals the stark contrast between abiding with the universe and living a life run on self-reliance and self-will. When we surrender, we feel grounded and one with the universe;

> *if you don't feel that—well, naturally, you feel alien, you feel a stranger in the world. And if you feel a stranger, you feel hostile. And therefore you start to bulldoze things about, to beat it up, and to try and make the world submit to your will.*[33]

This was the case with me. I was angry, strong-willed, and wanted things my way. I felt like a stranger in the world.

Certainly, I never understood what surrender meant until Gerry showed me what it looked like in my day-to-day interactions. Surrender is an abstract notion until it becomes an action. For example, when someone painfully says, "I am thirty-five years old; I wanted to be married by now; I wanted to have a family," we can relate. We can understand their frustration and disappointment. But from a spiritual perspective, it is clear that they are creating their own suffering, fueling their upset and fears, and resisting what is. They have *their* plan, *their* expectations, and they are sticking to them. They are not surrendering their will. They are not accepting what is.

To further demonstrate, when many years into my unself work I received the notice, "Carl, your services are no longer needed. Thank you for being part of our company," my response was surprisingly calm. Almost as if it wasn't me responding. The spiritual work asks me not to fuss about things not going *my* way. I can inquire as to why I was fired, but I listen without rebuttal and graciously accept their decision. Further, only when I am absent of ego and pride can I see and acknowledge the pain in the person who is the bearer of bad news. Moreover, seeing both sides of a situation lessens my chances of acting inappropriately, whereby doing so might eliminate any possibility of future employment with the company and with any affiliated company or person as well. When I trust what is, I *know* that whatever the outcome, I will be okay. I *know* that the universe knows best.

As Gerry used to say again and again, "God is everything or He's nothing." If our partner doesn't want to be with us any longer, if it's what they desire, if they have fallen out of love with us, we must go to understanding, compassion, and acceptance. We must open up our hearts to their pain, not just ours; otherwise, we create more suffering. As we grieve our loss, anger may come, as well as feelings of rejection and perhaps thoughts of retaliation. Come what may, we cannot feed the destructive thoughts and feelings nor act on them. We must turn it over to God, again and again.

When we surrender, we unearth the true meaning of patience, love, humility, and compassion. When we accept life on life's terms, we open up to grace. For grace is a by-product of surrender and acceptance. Over time, forgiveness comes, good wishes blossom, and we discover we are ready to let go and move on. At the start, walking on this path, we may see things as losses and rejections. But soon enough it becomes clear that the job we lost we really hated and the lover who left us wasn't right for us. In time, we come to know that "Rejection is God's protection," as the saying goes.

In any case, unless there is truly something we can do to change a situation, it is for our benefit to surrender to it and accept it. Resistance will only cause suffering.

> *Acceptance is the answer to all my problems today. When I am disturbed, it is because I find some person, place, thing, or situation—some fact of my life—unacceptable to me, and I can find no serenity until I accept that person, place, thing, or situation as being exactly the way it is supposed to be at this moment. Nothing, absolutely nothing, happens in God's world by mistake. ... Unless I accept life completely on life's terms, I cannot be happy. I need to concentrate not so much on what needs to be changed in the world as on what needs to be changed in me and in my attitudes.*[34]

From a spiritual standpoint, surrendering is a winning situation, not a losing one. We are not quitting; we are accepting what is, and we are letting go of the false belief that we are in control. The only fight we are giving up is the fight against the self.

A sober friend once put it so eloquently: "Whenever I go toe to toe with God, I lose." It is true, we will never win a fight against the laws of nature. Most certainly, whenever we rail against what is, we will suffer. But the will is strong and stubborn; it wants us to believe that we can rise above everything and conquer anything.

Back when I was struggling, still stubbornly pounding my hands whenever things didn't go *my* way, Gerry taught me that it was best not to have *a* way. However, refusing to give up control is understandable; giving up our control stirs up immense fear in us (more on fear in Chapters 10 and 15). After all, we are surrendering to something unseen and unknown to us. It requires a willingness and a great amount of faith and strength to surrender to something unperceived and mysterious—which is why it often takes a dire situation like a serious illness, deep depression, or great loss for us to surrender. And it's usually then, knowing that we are powerless, that we wake up to the reality of our situation: we are not in control. It's very difficult to admit that we are powerless. Yet the truth is, be it loss or sickness, be it tsunamis or viruses, we are powerless. Without doubt, the COVID-19 pandemic was proof of that. For sure, the invisible dangers are just as formidable as the earthquakes.

Prayer

In these types of dire situations, a large number of us customarily pray to God for certain outcomes. We believe that He will hear us and hopefully produce our desired results. But if the laws of nature are unalterable, how is this possible? Well, it's only possible when our will is in sync with the laws—God's will. Outside of that, praying for what *we* want is futile. In fact, praying for what *we* want is an act of self-will that rails against God. Practically speaking, in prayer, we are confronted with both self-will and God's will. In no uncertain terms, praying for anything other than *Thy will* is an action of non-surrendering, which is to say, if God is *what is*, there is only one prayer: "Thy will be done." Or, more specifically, "Thy will (not mine) be done."[35] Nevertheless, even with this knowledge, which can be found in most monotheistic religions and spiritual practices in some shape or form, a good number of us carry on praying for the things that *we* want.

Many of us thank God when He seems to answer our prayers and turn disappointed and disheartened when our prayers go unanswered. We plead to God during difficult times, resort to foxhole prayers when in despair, and bargain with the Almighty when we're fearful: "God, if you get me through this, I promise to never lie again." Yes, we are human: flawed and self-preserving, and when faced with a distressing situation, we are capable of doing anything to avoid emotional and physical pain. Even educated men and women of science who are atheists have been known to pray to God during bad turbulence when flying. It is natural to pray in desperate times. But in the end, we still have to accept what is, whether it's what we wished for or not.

You might exclaim, "Then why bother praying? Prayer seems pointless." Well, for one, praying for the willingness and strength to accept God's will, whatever the outcome, can be useful and effective.[36] With that being said, there is no harm in praying for what we desire, as long as we turn our will over to God. As a quote often attributed to author David R. Hawkins states, prayer is "holding in mind what you desire, but without adding desire to it."

The more we trust what is, the more directly we can tap into the reservoir of powerful resources within and beyond us, resources that we couldn't access otherwise. It is there, in trusting a God of our understanding, that we open ourselves up to grace. And so we pray, "God, grant me the serenity to accept the things I cannot change, the courage to change the things I can, and the wisdom to know the difference."[37]

Asking for Help

In the Twelve-Step Program of Alcoholics Anonymous, the sobriety circle-and-triangle symbol is powerful and meaningful. The triangle represents the three-part solution: unity, recovery, and service. The circle symbolizes the whole of AA: the program, fellowship, and sponsorship.[38] This is similar to the three-part solution in the Three Jewels in Buddhism: the Buddha, the dharma, and the sangha. Buddhists take refuge in the Buddha, which means to move forward toward surrendering to a higher consciousness. They take refuge in the dharma, which means to open our eyes to the teachings. And they take refuge in the sangha, which translates into a community of fellow practitioners who follow the path together, sharing one another's experiences.[39] Likewise, there is the three-part union of body, mind, and spirit in the Eight Limbs of Yoga.[40] Essentially, many of us cannot heal, recover, and align with our true nature and *what is* without outside teachings and help, hence the fellowship and sponsor in the Twelve-Step Program, the sangha and teacher in Buddhism, and the community and guru in Yoga. We cannot go it alone. We must seek help *and* ask for help.

A good number of us find it difficult, if not impossible, to ask for help. We are afraid of appearing weak, concerned that others will judge us if we reveal any signs of vulnerability. We want to look as though we have it all together, so we pretend that we are fine. But our life is somewhat of a façade. Fundamentally we are hiding a part of ourselves. Fear prevents us from realizing that asking for help is a sign of strength, wisdom, and our humanity.

If we get honest about it, outside of fear, I bet we'll find pride (which is fear-based). "I don't need help; I got this." "I can do this on my own." "I know what I need better than anyone else." "I'm a strong person; I can handle this." But "pride goeth before destruction."[41] Pridefulness is a dangerous mindset. When we cover up our true feelings and hide our vulnerability, we unknowingly push people away. And in our feelings of alienation and loneliness, we turn distrustful and destructive. Our view of the world becomes tainted. We hide things and we keep secrets. And as they say in AA, we're only as sick as our secrets.

Secrets separate us and burden us. Living with shameful secrets, hiding harms done, covering up for people who abuse us, allows the shame and guilt associated with the secrets to thrive and turn more powerful. When our unsound thoughts and behaviors remain shrouded in secrecy, they fester beneath the surface and sour into self-loathing and self-hatred. What's more, they cause immeasurable damage to others. Secrets make us sick and everyone around us sick.

What begins as low self-esteem turns to self-loathing and slowly burgeons into self-hate. We become hard on ourselves and perfectionistic, developing an inability to accept compliments and receive criticism well, while questioning the intentions of others. We become underachievers as a way to avoid mistakes and the disappointment of failure. Or conversely, we become overachievers to compensate for our lack of self-esteem, striving for excellence to prove our worth. Yet we can never be good enough.

Low self-esteem and self-loathing can localize into negative self-talk, although we are often unaware of this. *You're not talented enough to get that job. Stop being stupid; don't set yourself up for a big letdown. I can't believe I made that mistake again; I'm an idiot.* As these self-put-downs progressively get worse, our emphasis on negative occurrences slowly negates all the positive ones.

Back in my difficult and dark years, I was weighed down by depression and what seemed like the pain of the world. "King of Pain," a song by the rock group the Police, was my anthem. I sometimes thought of myself as akin to Jesus, on the cross, in pain, taking on the suffering of the world. But much later, I found out how wrong my association was; I was actually the antithesis of Jesus. In fact, I was more like Narcissus but in reverse. Instead of displaying self-love and vanity, I displayed self-hate and self-deprecation, which was just as egotistical and self-centered.

Learning to love ourselves takes a great deal of effort and patience, and it starts with asking for help, getting honest, and heightening our awareness. We must be watchful of our self-criticisms and self-deprecations, listening to our inner dialogue and taking note of how often we put ourselves down. Observing how we speak *to* ourselves and *about* ourselves while engaging with others is vital. More than that, we must stop verbalizing the negative commentary going on in our heads; verbalizing it only strengthens it. We keep the negativity alive and give it power when we believe it and let it become our identity. Gerry would often tell me, "Don't buy into the negative thoughts. Don't entertain them"—simple and practical advice that worked back then and still works today.

A willingness to be vulnerable makes us human. It opens us up to deeper, more loving relationships. It aligns us with our true nature and our Higher Power. But it can only be established by being honest and openhearted. It is a posture that Chögyam Trungpa calls the warrior stance, where one is fierce, strong, and brave yet compassionate, gentle, and humble. The warrior is not withholding, nor driven by fear. On the contrary, one draws courage from their vulnerability: "The ideal of warriorship is that the warrior should be sad and tender, and because of that, the warrior can be very brave as well."[42]

Our willingness to be vulnerable with others is affirming. It strengthens our trust in one another, which in turn deepens our relationships and encourages others to be more open with us. We need each other, and we connect more with each other when we are emotionally available and approachable. Everyone is better off when we ask for help.

To free ourselves from our *selves* and to connect with our Higher Power, we must break the silence, get honest, and shine the light on our dark secrets. Now, this doesn't mean we need to tell the world all our business. But we need at least one person who we can tell everything and anything to, someone we can trust. We can confide in a good friend, spelling out our intention, asking them if they are willing to listen and keep our confessions in confidence. We can explain to them that we are on a path of healing and that in order to move forward we have to free ourselves of things we have been holding inside. On the other hand, we might feel more comfortable opening up to a therapist or priest, or if we're in recovery, a sponsor. Whoever we choose, we have to be completely honest with them. It's the only way to liberate our souls.

Of course, this goes for depression, suicidal thinking, and any mental disorders as well. In my case, no one knew that I was suffering from these conditions. How would they? I kept them secret. And unbeknownst to me, my secrecy strengthened the symptoms, piqued the progression of the disease, and fed the shame I felt about them. I lived with these afflictions, believing they were unique to me. I thought I was alone, that I was strange, that something was terribly wrong with me, and others would find me crazy if they knew. Oddly, I didn't know others suffered from these same syndromes. And why was that? I was ignorant, unwise, uneducated, and unrevealing—I kept to myself. But luckily for me, I had a psychic breakdown. Consequently, I sought help.

When we open up to others, a connection takes place, a connection to others and our Higher Power. When we close up, we alienate ourselves, loneliness sets in, our thinking turns distorted, and we get sick, both physically and mentally. In the book *Buddha's Brain*, the authors urge us to be "feelable" if we want to "feel *felt*" and understood.[43] We have to open our hearts to our fellows and our Divine Power; otherwise, we will become spiritually ill. "According to one of the ayurvedic texts, the first and foremost cause of illness is the loss of faith in the divine."[44]

In his book *Walking with the Wind: A Memoir of the Movement*, the late US congressman John Lewis interprets St. Augustine: "Man is innately restless, forever restless, until he makes contact with God."[45] We cannot go it alone in life. Going to our Higher Power, fellowship, family, and friends for support is not a sign of weakness. It is a sign of strength and a gesture of our humanity. Of course, Gerry knew this more than anyone. When I was dealing with depression, isolating myself from everyone, fighting my demons, he kept at me: "Carl, you can't fight this battle alone. You gotta get God-strong." He would routinely deliver these words: "When two or more gather in the name of

God, the devil doesn't stand a chance." Asking for help is not a failing or symbol of defeat; it is a courageous act.

Undoubtedly, asking for help makes the world a better place, wherein everyone benefits.

We Have It Backward

When our effort is coming solely from self-will and willpower, our attempts at practicing patience, understanding, and tolerance remain frustratingly futile. These virtues are not available to us until we abide by the laws of nature. Of course we need to practice patience, although not for the sake of being patient but to humble ourselves to the fact that we are powerless over being patient. We have it backward. We don't strive for patience to be a better person; we humbly practice patience to connect with God.

Part of the problem is that our *will* and our *wanting* to be patient block us off from God (the laws of nature). We cannot *learn* how to be authentically patient. Fundamentally, we must stop trying, stop struggling, get out of our own way, and admit our powerlessness. Yes, we have to develop mind skills and behavioral skills, but genuine patience comes from the inside. Patience is within us, underneath the unwillingness, ego, cravings, and character flaws.

The same goes for gratitude. While working with Gerry, I remember him asking me to create a gratitude list. The notion was to make a list I could refer to whenever things went awry. Of course, I was to make it while I was in a good state of mind. But when I tried to create the list, it seemed forced and insincere, so I discarded the idea. I didn't believe it would help me anyway.

The following week I was deep in the sh*t, and Gerry asked me to get out my gratitude list. I told him I had no list. He asked why I didn't write one.

I angrily responded, "I don't care that I have two eyes, two legs, and a roof over my head. I don't want to live. I want to be dead. F*ck the gratitude list." This was where my self-hatred, anger, and depression took me—to a very dark and hopeless place. Understandably, Gerry disliked my resistance and ill-tempered reactions. Just the same, he never quit on me. He knew what it was like to be broken.

I truthfully didn't feel gratitude. Whether I was in the sh*t or not, gratitude was not a feeling I experienced, and I found it impossible to fake. I mean, how can one be grateful on purpose? This was why I found it impossible to subscribe to the self-help notion of cultivating gratitude. It didn't make sense to me (nor did any attempts at it work for me). But Gerry promised that by surrendering my *self* to a Power greater than myself, gratitude would come. And I trusted him.

It took a great amount of spiritual work before gratitude came to me. And not unlike patience, understanding, and tolerance, it came to me through grace. You see, I believe that our view and experience of God rests on us. That is to say, the God we experience depends on how we view ourselves, others, and the world. If we hate ourselves, we will hate people, the planet, and existence itself. And naturally, we will hate and renounce God. Again, we have it backward. We must learn to love ourselves before we can learn to love others.

Once we do the inside work and surrender our will and our short-comings, the channel to our Source of Consciousness opens up and everything begins to fall into place. Once we align with our true nature, everything starts to come together. And by way of divine connection, we gain the power we lack and *become* patient, understanding, and tol-erant. We *become* grateful. We *become* complete. And we *become* whole.

CHAPTER SEVEN

Curbing the Craving for More

When I was deep into my addictions, I searched everywhere
for cures, solutions, and answers, never thinking that my
problem might be an internal, spiritual one.

I remember how drinking alcohol once produced feelings that I mistook for equanimity and peace. Of course, this was long before alcohol nearly destroyed me. In "The Doctor's Opinion," Dr. William Silkworth writes, "Men and women drink essentially because they like the effect produced by alcohol."[46] And this was why I drank—and drank and drank and drank: for the effect—for that feeling of transcendence. I experienced the "spiritual" by voyaging in the strong waters—alcohol. It sent me sailing into oblivion. It obliterated my ego—at least temporarily. But unlike true transcendence, it didn't lighten my journey. No, the drink dragged me under and nearly drowned my soul.

In his book *The Pastor: A Memoir*, Eugene Peterson untangles the connection between addiction and spirituality: "Classically, there are three ways in which humans try to find transcendence ... apart from God ...: through the ecstasy of alcohol and drugs, through the ecstasy of recreational sex, through the ecstasy of crowds."[47]

These indulgences may seem to ease our suffering and connect us to the divine. But they don't. They keep us from doing the spiritual work and prevent us from experiencing true transformation. They feed the self, which drives us toward these cravings, in search of an external fix to an internal problem.

Alcoholism and Drug Addiction

Long before sobriety, I didn't know what an alcoholic was, let alone alcoholism. As I mentioned earlier, my image of the alcoholic was a conventional one. It was the bum on the street brown-bagging a pint of cheap whiskey and the old man wobbling home from the pub late at night, not the successful entrepreneur or the lonely housewife starving for company.

Alcoholism is not based on appearance, nor on economic status, class, race, religion, gender, or education. It does not discriminate. Alcoholism is a disease of which drinking alcohol is but a symptom. We can look at it this way: When we remove *alcohol* from *alcoholism*, we are left with the *ism*. And this *ism* is why an alcoholic drinks, a drug addict uses, a gambler gambles, a shopaholic shops, and a workaholic works. An accurate acronym (often heard in the rooms of AA) that defines this *ism* is *internal spiritual malady*. Simply put, the symptoms are addictive behaviors, self-centeredness, negative thinking, a deep-seated restlessness, irritability, and discontentment. Of course, this creates suffering, suffering that can only be assuaged through the spiritual work.

When I put down the drink for good, I thought my troubles were over. But I discovered quickly that without the drink to fall back on, I was at a loss as to how to handle my emotions. When I was sad, I desired an inebriant. When I was riding high, celebrating an achievement, I wanted to reward myself with an intoxicating beverage. Whenever I got angry, I wanted to booze it up. Early in my sobriety, I recall one night having a fight with my lover. As I sat steaming with frustration and anger, she poured herself a glass of wine. I shouted at her, "You are so lucky that you can drink." I stormed out of the apartment, slamming the door. The urge to go to a bar or a liquor store was mighty. As I walked down the street, I kicked a few trash cans before coming upon a convenience store. I purchased a tub of ice cream, sat on the curb, and ate it all. That was all I could think of doing.

As the months passed, every reason as to why I drank introduced itself to me. Emotions erupted from deep within me. I could no longer drown them in alcohol or numb them with drugs. I thought my problem with alcohol was simply that I was drinking too much. But to my utter surprise, something shockingly profound was unveiling itself to me—deep unprocessed emotions, the absence of coping mechanisms, and my *alcoholic mind*—the *isms* (internal spiritual malady).

When I was deep into my addictions, I searched everywhere for cures, solutions, and answers, never thinking that my problem might be an internal, spiritual one. Indeed, as was revealed to me, I was living my life as a dry drunk, which is to say I put down the drink, but I wasn't treating the *isms*. I learned that when an alcoholic puts down the drink, he or she remains an alcoholic until they treat the *disease*. You could say I was abstinent but not sober.

I remained pessimistic, negative, cynical, distrusting, and easily triggered. I was self-absorbed, selfish, easily offended, and emotionally sensitive and immature. I was still suffering from anger issues, depression, debilitating anxiety, and suicidal tendencies. My tone and attitude toward people were harsh and pugnacious. I would walk away from a heated exchange that I had initiated, thinking, "What the f*ck is their problem?" I was reactive and had no *pause* button. I was unable to handle difficult and challenging situations well. I routinely shut down emotionally and isolated myself. I alienated people. I blamed others for all my problems. But to be clear, although these are some of the common characteristics of an alcoholic, all human beings possess them to one degree or another.

All the same, I had little hope of being free from the desire to drink until I dealt with the *isms*. Yes, as long as I remained a dry drunk, the fear and risk of picking up again would persist. Moreover, as I later discovered, I didn't stand a chance of alleviating my suffering and finding happiness while under the influence of alcohol. So, I had to stay dry and do the unself work.

I remember when I started working with Gerry, whenever the cravings came on strong, he would say, "Play the tape out to the end, Carl." Meaning, think it through before picking up, and think about the consequences of having that first drink. When I did, it became plain that it wouldn't end well. For certain, the regret, remorse, guilt, shame, and self-loathing I would experience picking up again would drag me down into the depths of self-hate. Gerry would say that once you order that drink and put your money on the bar, you may as well put your house keys, car keys, and driver's license on the bar too. Yes, contrary to the drunkard's belief, when an alcoholic decides to drink, they don't "lose" their house, car, license, and marriage; they give them away. Without question, something had to be done about my cravings.

The *isms*—the restlessness, irritability, and discontentment, and the anxiety that accompanies them—begin long before one picks up their first drink, places their first bet, binge shops for the first time, or works that first seventy-hour workweek that leaves them exhausted but charged. Culturally, in the West, alcohol is commonly introduced to us as a solution to our unease, as a way to de-stress. And for many, that first drink is like coming home. For others, this is not so much the case. Here lies the distinction between the alcoholic and nonalcoholic—for the former, alcohol works! As for the latter, they don't find relief from alcohol in the same way. It might calm and relax them, but it doesn't transform them as it does for the alcoholic. The same goes for drugs and others substances.

To gain a glimpse of the power of alcohol over the alcoholic, I'll share an experience of when this power became apparent to me. One evening at a club in a lively part of town, my date and I were seated at a table ordering drinks. The club was crowded, there was live music, and the night was young. I remember feeling claustrophobic and cautious of my surroundings. When our drinks arrived, I anxiously but slowly took a sip of my whiskey. As that familiar and delightful burn coated my throat, a warm tingle that began at the top of my head slowly glided down my body to my toes. In an instant, the club magically transformed from a crowded place to a cozy one. The clubgoers turned convivial and cordial. The band sounded smooth and groovy, and my date looked comfy, warm, sweet, and sexy. A smile emerged from my mouth, welcoming this euphoric state. Life was good. I was comfortable in my skin. Nothing on the outside had changed, yet the world revamped itself into a friendlier place.

It is no mere coincidence that liquor is referred to as spirits. In fact, for the alcoholic, the effect of alcohol is a spiritual experience—it changes something on the inside, even if short-lived. And it's a fix that the alcoholic constantly craves, where "one is too many, and a thousand not enough," a sentiment often heard in the recovery rooms of AA. Sadly, alcohol only brings temporary relief; it is not a cure. It is an ersatz enlightenment, not nirvana. Although the drink may lift us up, in the end, it will knock us down in prostration to the porcelain god.

Upon my first taste of alcohol, it felt like I found a magical cure. My anxieties and worries dissipated, and I became comfortable in my skin. That is, until alcohol started depleting me and destroying my body, mind, and spirit. Alcohol is a depressant, and it was definitely a contributing factor, if not the primary cause, of my chronic depression. As long as I maintained a romance with the moonshine, depression would remain my drinking companion. But back when I was drinking heavily, I didn't believe there was any correlation. My *alcoholic mind* and depression skewed my view of reality and the world. It colored it a dark gray and kept me in *self* and in my head. I saw life as absurd and meaningless. Alcohol was distorting my mind, advancing my unease, alienating and isolating me from the rest of the world, and blocking me from a Power greater than myself. I was suffering spiritually and needed to connect to others and my divine nature.

Eugene Peterson nailed it—transcendence is what we crave—only, as I previously mentioned, we don't know it. The neurosciences concur. In *How God Changes Your Brain*, authors Newberg and Waldman claim, "As doctors, we have come to realize that people need to deal with their spiritual pathology in addition to their physical and mental concerns."[48]

Sex Addiction

Let me begin first with a disclaimer: Any moralistic views on sex are beyond the scope of the subject at hand. My intention is not to judge anyone's sexual proclivities, nor is my objective an ethical one. I simply want to show how sex addiction stems from the same malady as alcoholism and that "the ecstasy of recreational sex," as outlined by Peterson, is just another erroneous way some of us seek transcendence.

Sex is a delicate and complicated subject. What we can say for certain is that we are sexual beings. But we must get honest about sex, both with ourselves and in our relations. And we can start by exploring and investigating our habits, thoughts, and feelings about sex. Talk therapy could be the best way to begin the process of self-discovery. We can also practice Yoga as a way to unearth deeply embedded feelings (see Chapter 10). Taking up a meditation practice can certainly shed light on our troubles, helping reveal the reasons behind them (see Chapter 8). And, of course, praying for wisdom and guidance can help cut to the chase. These are the steps we can take to help empower ourselves and liberate ourselves from the chains that bind us and cause us grief. Taking these steps helped me discover that my sexual tendencies pointed to the same *isms* as alcohol.

My sexual problems and biased beliefs were strongly associated with my Catholic surroundings. The messages I received during my upbringing were complex and bewildering—sex is impure; sexual thoughts are unclean; masturbation is a sin. "Watch and pray so that you will not fall into temptation. The spirit is willing, but the flesh is weak."[49] When sex (consciously or subconsciously) is viewed this way, rest assured, feelings of guilt and shame will arise.

In America, the nude body has been a cause of shame. Nakedness has been eroticized and sexualized to the point that it is essentially viewed as carnal. The idea that nudity is naughty can be traced back to our American forebears, the Puritans. Their religious moral attitudes have made it nearly impossible for us to separate nudity from sex. This unhealthy mindset is fear-based, and it's married to shame and guilt. In the West, as adolescents many of us had to hide our wonder about nudity and sex. We were coerced to obscure and suppress our sexual impulses and desires. And we had little choice but to succumb to the stigma and shame attached to our thoughts and cravings. Sex was sinful and unclean, yet it was also mysterious and exciting. Undeniably, early experiences of nudity and sex set many of us off course, navigating us into disturbing habits and debilitating beliefs, taboos, fears, and myths about sex. In days past, as teenagers we curiously and covertly ogled porn magazines in the back of newspaper and magazine stores. Some of us may have snuck into peep shows, strip joints, and brothels. Today, many youngsters and adults alike hide in their rooms, cars, or offices and view internet porn whenever they want, for free.

A common but rarely talked about cause of sexual addiction, particularly with men, pertains to the implicit promise that sex will provide them with the very things they were culturally taught to stifle—intimacy, sensuality, passion, and the release of emotions like sadness and hurt. Most men in the West are conditioned early on to conform to a limited idea of masculinity. They are raised to conceal and repress their emotions. "Real men" are taught to be strong. "Real men" don't cry. And so sex becomes the sole outlet for their repressed emotions and a way to escape their daily stoic, mundane lives. However, sex cannot fulfill all of their needs, so they become both disappointed and dissatisfied, not knowing that their issues actually lie in the deprivation of their humanity. Namely, that they had to, and still have to, publicly pretend that all is well at school or work, with friends, with their families, and socially. Essentially, these men are living a lie, and so they seek transcendence through sex.

Generally, during sex, both men and women seem to rise above thought and material existence and travel far beyond normal experience. The orgasm is like an out-of-body episode, like a "little death," as the French say. In fact, sex can be much like a spiritual experience. It's no wonder why the orgasm has been referred to as both heaven and ether in literature. Yet, unlike platonic love, which is a love that ascends above romantic love and sexual passion to a higher love and ideal, sex as a sole way to experience intimacy and transcendence is not unlike alcohol in that it will leave you high and dry and craving more and more.

We can begin by asking ourselves some basic questions. "Am I obsessed with sex?" "Are my sexual behaviors an issue?" "Are they causing myself and others harm?" "Have they had serious and damaging consequences?" "Are sex and sex-seeking taking up a lot space in my head?" "Has sex with my partner become less frequent because of pornography?" "Has sex become solely fetishistic?" "Am I just living out my pornographic fantasies with others?" "Do I objectify women or men?" "Has sex become purely masturbatory?" "Have my sexual behaviors become just another form of escape?" "Has sex become my only outlet for intimacy, sensuality, and love and the sole source of vulnerability, passion, companionship, and relaxation?" "Has sex become the only time I really feel my body and emotions?"

Sex addiction has severe consequences. We only have to look at the people who seem to have it all yet ruin their lives by impulsively and insidiously sleeping around with others. People with good educations, successful careers, financial wealth, fame, celebrity, clout, beautiful partners, healthy children, and lavish homes destroy their lives over their uncontrollable sexual desire. This is addiction, and even wealth and prestige cannot cure it. Nothing on the outside can remedy it. Like alcoholism, sex addiction does not discriminate. Whether we are rich and famous or a working-class member of society, on the inside we are all the same. No one is immune to the *isms*. We are all susceptible to becoming enslaved to our sexual desires.

Some get caught up in a vicious cycle of sexual misconduct, obsessively seeking sex as a way to escape increasingly ill feelings about their dishonest and uncontrollable behavior. They suppress their feelings of guilt, shame, remorse, and regret and grow dependent on a constant consumption of sex in order to feel good about themselves. Recreational sex is how they transcend their pain, loneliness, and suffering. But no single person can meet their demands; their sexual appetite is insatiable. I sampled a long list of proclivities for far too long—which made monogamy impossible and conventional sex colorless. I needed a lot of diversity and stimulation. My escapades throughout the years were outrageous, risky, and outright dangerous, not to mention harmful. I slept with just about anyone who was willing. I couldn't stop myself. I couldn't help myself. And I couldn't stand myself. The guilt, shame, and remorse grew into an aggressive cancer, spreading and ravaging my soul. I felt like a lowlife. And perhaps I was one.

There came a time when I hit a breaking point. I knew I couldn't continue living the way I was living. I tried everything imaginable to control my sky-high sexual cravings and to succeed in romance and sex relations. I attempted monogamy over and over, but with few exceptions, I was unable to remain faithful and committed for very long. I tried casual affairs and multiple partners. I did this covertly at first, but my conscience got the best of me, so I tried to be open and honest about my outside affairs with women, yet this only hurt them. Nothing worked.

I tried celibacy for a time in the hopes that I would discover some insight in the absence of sex. As it turned out, I painfully did. I learned that without affection, without being touched, and without a warm body to hold me, I began withering away. Without having sex in my life, I felt deprived and achingly hollow.

Years later, while working with Gerry, the spiritual way of living slowly started showing the cause of my troubles. Outside of my neediness and cravings, which were beginning to dissipate, it became apparent that I objectified women. Granted, I had many women friends who I respected and saw as equals, but another side of me sexually objectified the women outside of that circle. And this view of women charged my libido, which was a necessary evil—how else could I transcend my emotional pain and suffering, especially without alcohol and substances no longer in my life? So, it goes without saying, if I was to stop viewing women as objects, pornography had to be the first thing to go. I already knew I was addicted to porn. I had tried stopping many times. But like my early experiences in trying to control my drinking, I would abstain from viewing porn for a while but then give into it again. I would binge-watch until I had to quit cold turkey again. I knew it was a negative habit I had to give up.

Far more than that, I had to refrain from flirting with women and fantasizing about them. Instead, I focused on being friendly with them as a way to stop objectifying them. If there was any sexual flirtation or mystique at the start, I would end it quickly by immediately puncturing it with an honest heart-to-heart conversation. What's more, I stopped twisting my neck each time a pretty woman passed me on the street—one glance, if that, and I would walk on. These were the efforts I made. And of course, I failed again and again.

Over time, albeit slowly, as I focused on unselfing and surrendering my selfish desires to a Higher Power, change began to come. When we give up greedy pleasure-seeking and face the source of our cravings and deepest fears, then positive change appears. "Our thought-life will be placed on a much higher plane when our thinking is cleared of wrong motives."[50]

The Right Ideal About Sex

Gerry and I didn't talk much about women and sex. In fact, other than going through the pen-to-paper work on sex harms and helping me repair my relationship with my partner at the time, we spoke little about sex. Which reminds me... I never got around to asking him about the tattoo on the crown of his head, although I do recall overhearing a guy once say that it was a vulva. At least that's my recollection. I also have memories of Gerry saying during a few meetings (while pointing to his head) that this is what happens when you get drunk.

My kinship with Gerry was turning into a brotherly friendship. We were hanging out quite a bit. We often met up at a local diner after a meeting. Sometimes we splurged and dined at a fancier place. We talked about the recovery work, God, and our professional lives. Gerry had his own business. He did construction. He built things like counters, cabinets, and ceilings. He took pride in his work and no doubt loved it, although not as much as dancing. He loved to dance. And he was good at it. He liked to get dressed up on occasion and go to a club. But I must say, his wardrobe was... well, colorful and dated. Gerry was a late-'70s throwback. A night out consisted of a color-coordinated outfit—jacket; satin shirt with the collar over the lapels, upper buttons undone; gold chains; flared trousers; and freshly polished shoes. He was always clean and well-groomed. On one cold night, we planned to drive to an out-of-town club. When I honked my car horn outside his house, he walked out in a white, fluffy, faux-fur coat. It was bold and classic. Pure Gerry. He definitely stood out in a crowd.

I know Gerry struggled with women, love, and sex. Like me, he adored the love and attention of women and had an inordinate craving for sex. Still, I trusted he was working on it as I was. Currently, as I continue on the road to change, I'm learning how to strive toward more lovemaking and less fantasy-like sex in my monogamous relationships. Whereas I used to need a lot of stimulation, I can now have conventional sex and stay in the moment.

With a healthy-minded view about sex, it can be natural, positive, intimate, loving, and pleasurable. When we experience sex as a gift, the orgasm becomes a celebration, provided we aspire to experience something resembling a platonic love. I'm reminded of a wonderful quote often attributed to Marvin J. Ashton: "Pleasure usually takes the form of me and now; joy is us and always."

Finding a balance between love, romance, sex, family, friendships, and work, which was never attainable before, has made my life full. Monogamy comes naturally, which has made my life a lot less complicated and eased my suffering. Unquestionably, the freedom that comes from living without unhealthy sexual cravings is beyond measure. How liberating it is to not want to sleep with every woman who smiles at me.

"To sum up about sex: We earnestly pray for the right ideal, for guidance in each questionable situation, for sanity, and for the strength to do the right thing."[51]

Attention, Applause, Praise, and Reward

To one extent or another, we all delight in receiving praise for our hard work and accomplishments. But we must be watchful, for "the ecstasy of crowds," as Peterson phrased it, can turn addictive. Especially if we suffer from the *isms*. Examining the social media platforms, it is apparent that the *like* button provides a feel-good fix that quickly turns this reward system into an addictive behavior.

Although not as intense as [a] hit of cocaine, positive social stimuli will similarly result in a release of dopamine, reinforcing whatever behavior preceded it. Cognitive neuroscientists have shown that rewarding social stimuli—laughing faces, positive recognition by our peers, messages from loved ones—activate the same dopaminergic reward pathways. Smartphones have provided us with a virtually unlimited supply of social stimuli, both positive and negative. Every notification, whether it's a text message, a "like" on Instagram, or a Facebook notification, has the potential to be a positive social stimulus and dopamine influx.[52]

As Gerry would say, we are "feel-good junkies," and some will post just about anything online in an effort to increase dopamine to the brain. Some post outrageous videos of themselves performing great (sometimes risky) gymnastic feats. Others share sexually provocative pictures for public viewing. It all becomes a seductive game of how many *like*s one can accumulate. For many, reaching the highest numbers of likes, friends, and followers becomes of utmost importance.

A concerning number of people want to be noticed, seen, and famous. Many have turned into their own picture-taking paparazzi, posting and documenting most every move they make. Whether it be at home, school, work, or out on a date, they post it for the world to see. Not unlike in a tabloid paper, their private lives have become front-page news, or at least that's the fantasy.

Why do we seek attention and applause? Yes, it makes us feel good to be complimented and acknowledged for our achievements, but what else is at work? Perhaps we are seeking the approval that we never received from our parents. Or could it be that we were praised and rewarded so often for our accomplishments as a child that we have become dependent on recognition and a pat on the back? Or is it because external validation enables us to break free from the discomfort of self-doubt? Whatever the reason, our strong cravings for attention and praise cause us to suffer.

In *The Next Frontier: Emotional Sobriety*, the author, Bill Wilson, a cofounder of Alcoholics Anonymous, shares how after several years of spiritual development, he belatedly came to realize the root cause of his addiction, recurring depression, unease, and unhappiness: "false dependencies." He writes, "Those adolescent urges that so many of us have for top approval, perfect security, and perfect romance—urges quite appropriate to age seventeen—prove to be an impossible way of life when we are at age forty-seven or fifty-seven."[53] When we base our self-value on the opinions of others, turning to them to feel good about ourselves, we become reliant on their good word, summoning attention, praise, love, and a steady flow of accolades and approval. We turn gravely dependent on them, craving a constant supply of love and adoration to feel good enough, talented enough, smart enough, and successful enough. And over time, our hunger for compliments and handclapping grows and grows, which blinds us from seeing the harm it is causing others and ourselves: "For my dependency meant demand—a demand for the possession and control of the people and the conditions surrounding me."[54] Wilson writes,

> *My basic flaw had always been dependence—almost absolute dependence—on people or circumstances to supply me with prestige, security, and the like. ... I found I had to exert every ounce of will and action to cut off these faulty emotional dependencies ... Plainly, I could not avail myself of God's love until I was able to offer it back to Him by loving others as He would have me. And I couldn't possibly do that so long as I was victimized by false dependencies.*[55]

Wilson came to understand the true meaning of the adage "It is better to give than to receive."[56] He writes, "My stability came out of trying to give, not out of demanding that I receive."[57]

66

When we give, "happiness is a by-product—the extra dividend of giving without any demand for a return."[58] As we surrender our selfish needs and help others (in effect, unself), our reliance on attention and praise weakens and our craving for compliments wanes. In consequence, when acclaim and kudos do come our way, we can welcome them with gratitude and humbleness, not from a yearning for validation.

Purpose and Meaning

I met a gentleman at a recovery meeting a few years back who was a successful owner of a well-established and thriving company. He had accumulated great financial wealth. He was physically fit and married with three healthy children. Yet he was lugubrious and miserably unhappy. I remember him saying to me that the reason for his unhappiness was that he wasn't as rich as Bill Gates. I thought, *Why would he set the bar so high and use Bill Gates as a reference point?*

While reflecting on our interaction, I was reminded of something I read only a few weeks prior. It may be antiquated, but it's apropos:

> *Practically every boy in the United States dreams of becoming our President. … As he gets older and sees the impossibility of this, he can smile good-naturedly at his childhood dream. … In later life he finds that real happiness is not to be found in just trying to be a number one man … . He's still ambitious, but not absurdly so.*[59]

After becoming more acquainted with my forlorn friend in recovery, it became apparent he was still a child in some sense. It also turned evident that while he had purpose in his life—to be richer—his life lacked meaning. For the alcoholic "may not be able to stay sober, or even alive, unless he passes on to other alcoholics what was so freely given him."[60]

If our purpose in life lacks meaning, whether we succeed in our endeavors or not, in the end, we will never be satisfied. Indeed, our accomplishments can never bring us true fulfillment. The hope and expectation that something or someone will bring us lasting joy and happiness is a false one, for the thrill of our achievements will fleetly fade, letting us down and leaving us wanting more. Until we do the inside work, until we find purpose *and* meaning, we will always feel a lack.

I remember another speaker in recovery telling us how he had asked a friend who had amassed huge amounts of money if the money changed anything. His friend replied by saying, "To be honest, I was on my yacht the other night thinking about killing myself."

Money, material things, and accolades are nice, but they cannot take away our underlying angst and dissatisfaction in life. Without purpose and meaning, peace and happiness will remain elusive. Yes, we can strive for success, excellence, and mastery, for living our dreams in and of itself is what is purposeful, whether we achieve our goals or not. But a purposeful dream that also benefits others is what ultimately brings meaning to our lives. We become part of something bigger, and we transcend the self.

CHAPTER EIGHT

Rewiring the Mind

We mustn't let the self have its way. We mustn't quit,
even though our minds try to convince us otherwise.

Our mind thinks; that's what it does. We cannot stop thoughts from arising. It's our attachment to them that causes a lot of our suffering. It's our inability to let them go that deflects us from focusing, relaxing, and sleeping at night. It's our overthinking and over-analyzing that is the cause of our anxieties and unease. From time to time, I half-jokingly tell my students, "If you want to be happy, stop thinking." Of course, you can't stop thinking, but you don't have to be enslaved by every thought that appears. I learned that unwanted, distracting, and obsessive thoughts are not the problem. It's actually the way we respond to the thoughts, and our relationship to them, that cause suffering. The practice of meditation can transform that relationship. Imagine being able to literally take this suggestion: *Don't give it another thought.* Meditation gives us that gift freely.

If the mention of meditation makes you roll your eyes, I understand. I was skeptical too. In fact, I had no desire to try it, no interest in it, no time for it, and I couldn't see how it could possibly help me. How could sitting still in a seated position doing nothing have any benefits? It made no practical sense. All the same, the universe had other plans for me. As part of my Yoga teaching training program, I had to study *and* practice Buddhist meditation.

The Buddha came to know that the mind is ill at ease being in the present moment. This is one reason why meditation is burdensome in the beginning. The mind is easily distracted and loves to wander, fantasize, relive the past, plan, plot, and worry. Buddhists call this "monkey mind." As a monkey jumps from one branch to another, so does the mind jump from one thought to another. Meditation trains our minds to be more steady, present, focused, and aware.

The Neuroscience of Meditation

Experts in the neuroscientific community are making extraordinary discoveries about the benefits of meditation and prayer. Through the use of real-time MRI and functional MRI (fMRI) technologies and brain imaging, they have collected a considerable amount of convincing data. Their findings show that living a spiritual or religious way of life can help heal the brain and substantially improve one's quality of life (less suffering equals more happiness).

Neuroscientist Richard Davidson, professor of psychology and psychiatry and the founding director of the Waisman Laboratory for Brain Imaging and Behavior, is known for his profound work studying the brain. In an interview entitled "Emotion Regulation and Dysregulation," Davidson speaks about the amygdala, the section of the brain responsible for emotions like anger and fear and for regulating aggression.

> If we're confronted with a stress, we often have an emotional reaction that perseverates, that just goes on beyond the point where it's useful ... One of the things that we found is that practicing mindfulness [meditation] will actually lead to faster recovery in the amygdala; the amygdala comes back down to baseline more quickly.[61]

That is to say, the practice of meditation will bring about a faster recovery time from heated emotions such as anger and prevent stress from spilling over into ensuing experiences. He says that mindfulness "doesn't change the response itself, but what it does seem to do, is it changes how quickly you recover."[62] Additionally, research done by Adrienne A. Taren and her colleagues shows a correlation between mindfulness and improvements in how one reacts to stress. Their studies also show how long-term mindfulness meditation practice significantly decreases the size of the amygdala in physical volume.[63]

That's the good news. The bad news is that our culture tends to increase the size of the amygdala, in a manner of speaking. The media bombards us with daily dosages of misdemeanors, murders, and mayhem, reliably supplying us with the fodder that fuels our fears. This strengthens our distrust of others, keeping us on guard, anticipating danger, and perceiving people and situations as potential threats. The media plays us, baits us, hooks us, and lights up the flames of aggression that arouse us to fiercely fire away on social media, at work, and at home.

Entrepreneur Peter H. Diamandis insightfully breaks it down for us: "Bad news sells because the amygdala is always looking for something to fear."[64] In order to sell newspapers and get high ratings, the media administers fear, perpetually providing us with potential problems to worry about. This narrow view of reality can morph our perception, turning the world into a fearful, ugly place; mutating people into distorted and threatening alien beings; and transforming us into aggressive, defensive protectors of our like-minded groups.

Whatever the source, negative input can be damaging to our neural circuitry and harmful to our bodies. This is apparent in an article published in the *British Journal of Psychology*:

Participants who watched the negatively valenced bulletin showed increases in both anxious and sad mood, and also showed a significant increase in the tendency to catastrophize a personal worry. The results are consistent with those theories of worry that implicate negative mood as a causal factor in facilitating worrisome thought. They also suggest that negatively valenced TV news programmes can exacerbate a range of personal concerns that are not specifically relevant to the content of the programme.[65]

For some, an hour of news and political commentary each night and thirty minutes of social media per day may be easy to keep in check. For others, though, like those of us in recovery, achieving an equilibrium can be challenging, if not impossible. Considering that, abstinence might be the better alternative.

Whatever alternative you choose, meditation can help minimize worry and mend the neural pathways of your brain. Meditation can be thought of as mental hygiene for the mind. Just as the physical body will decline without good nutrition, exercise, and rest, the mind will malfunction without meditation and mindfulness. Stanford brain surgeon and author James Doty writes:

Just like muscles, our mental muscle, if you will, responds to exercise. It's just which exercise you're going to do. And one exercise relates to mindfulness, compassion, loving-kindness, having an open heart. And when you strengthen that muscle, the world becomes a vibrant place where you recognize the incredible aspect of humanity that surrounds you in every person ... Or you can do a form of exercise that makes you afraid, that makes you pull away, that makes you think that people are your enemies .... Unfortunately ... for many people, they don't even understand that this is happening.[66]

However, meditation can wake us up to this understanding. Further, a regular meditation practice can lift our spirits, gifting us with positive feelings of hope and well-being. In their book *How God Changes Your Brain*, Newberg and Waldman cite a study about the significant positive effects of meditation:

A 65 percent increase in dopamine was found when individuals practiced yoga nidra, a form of meditation in which a person maintains conscious awareness while remaining in a state of complete relaxation. Dopamine heightens sensory imagery, generates pleasurable experiences, stimulates positive thoughts, increases your sense of well-being, and allows you to feel safe in the world. Even the high that results from cocaine is related directly to the sudden increase of dopamine in the brain. This may explain why some people equate spiritual experiences with drug experiences, since both share common pathways in the brain.[67]

The sciences are unquestionably showing the profits from a daily meditation practice, but the brain is a mysterious organ, and many will doubt its efficacy. Certainly, skepticism has its place. Cynicism, on the other hand, is an entirely different animal. And cynics tend to be masterful procrastinators. But meditation is an action. Indeed, researching it, studying it, pondering it, and debating it are important, but for it to work, we must put it into practice.

Practice

With regular practice, our bodies get more comfortable and relaxed, our minds get quieter, and we become less attached to our thoughts. We transform into observers of our own thoughts, watching and noticing how the mind has a mind of its own. We come to find that we are not in control of our thoughts; we are, in fact, powerless over them. As we gain insight as to how the mind functions, we learn to accept its unpredictability. If the mind is filled with random thoughts, we can step back, let them be, and watch them from afar, from a quieter place. Meditation heightens our self-awareness. We get acquainted with our minds more intimately. We get to know ourselves. What serves us and what doesn't is revealed. The wisdom, intelligence, intuition, and power within us emerge. We come to *know*.

At the start of a meditation practice, we shouldn't be alarmed; sitting quietly in our bodies with our thoughts, feelings, and emotions will be difficult at first. We will experience physical and mental discomfort. Things are going to come up that will agitate us. The inner chatter and internal monologue will be disturbing at times. A self-defeating voice may appear. *I can't do this; I'm not capable. This is not for me. This meditation stuff is just nonsense.* We mustn't buy into these thoughts. We mustn't let the self have its way. We mustn't quit, even though our minds try to convince us otherwise.

Meditation was extremely difficult for me at first. Actually, it was torturous. I could not sit still. My body would cramp, ache, and spasm. I had to constantly shift and stretch. The physical unease, anxiety, and tension were too much to bear. On top of that, my mind wouldn't quiet down. The racing thoughts in my head wouldn't stop. My body and mind refused to relax and calm down. Suffice to say, of all the spiritual disciplines, seated meditation was the most difficult for me. It took years to incorporate it into my daily practice of unselfing. In hindsight, there was a hump I had to get over, a physical and emotional detox I needed to go through, which took a lot of time and patience.

In seated meditation, there is no escaping the self, so we have to work with it. Viewing our unwanted thoughts, feeling our imposing feelings, and sitting with our uncomfortable bodily sensations is part of the practice. If we stick with it, we will witness changes and shifts soon enough. The self-critic (who speaks to us more often than we may have realized) will pressingly present itself in all its glory while we go about our day. *I screwed up again. I'm not smart enough. I'm getting old, and I'm going to end up being alone.* Other surprising shortcomings will surface that we had little or no awareness of, such as how frequently we judge and criticize others. *Look at that dress! I can't believe she thinks she looks good in it! She's so naïve. My brother is a loser; he just can't get it together.* These thoughts may bring up feelings of guilt. But this is a good thing; it gives us the chance to work with our thoughts, feelings, and flaws. As they come into the light, they lose their power and become more manageable.

In his book *The Power of Now*, Eckhart Tolle describes what can change through witnessing our own consciousness:

> *So when you listen to a thought, you are aware not only of the thought but also of yourself as the witness of the thought. A new dimension of consciousness has come in. As you listen to the thought, you feel a conscious presence—your deeper self—behind or underneath the thought, as it were.*[68]

As we practice meditation, we develop mind skills. We learn to watch our thoughts as though we were a scientist in a lab clinically examining someone else's mind. By understanding that we are not our thoughts, we yield an objectivity wherein we can view our thoughts, however bothersome they might be, and remain relaxed and calm. Steve Hickman, PsyD, describes what a head full of thoughts can feel like and how meditation can help: "People with anxiety tend to feel their thoughts are coming at them like a waterfall. Open monitoring [meditation] allows you to stand in the quiet space behind the waterfall and watch your thoughts but not be pummeled by them."[69]

The Waterfall Meditation[70] that follows is a simple and effective meditation to try as a beginner. It's based on various meditations. Sitting comfortably on the floor or in a chair with your spine straight and tall, breathing naturally in and out of the nose, close your eyes, and...

Waterfall Meditation

Imagine a waterfall. Visualize the water cascading down to the rapids below it. Think of the falling water as your thoughts. We can practice mindfulness by going behind the waterfall to that quiet space in the cavity in the rock. From there, we can view the water, safe from the gushing deluge. We can watch the water—namely, our thoughts—and allow a distance between them and witness-consciousness. In this space, we can cultivate mindfulness. Imagine yourself there, observing the water. Breathe. Be still. The noise of the pummeling water is a distance away. There is a gap between you (the watcher) and all the noise. This quiet place is within you, behind the noise in your head. Be still. Hear the silence. It's always there. It's constant. You can always go there. It awaits you. Sit there now and breathe quietly for five minutes.

With regular practice, clingy, distracting, and overwhelming thoughts stick less and pass more freely. The body relaxes, the mind quiets down, and our suffering eases.

Negative Thoughts and Emotions

As I practiced meditation, my awareness of my distressing thoughts throughout the day increased. I began to notice that every negative thought left a residue of unease in my body. This first came to my attention while shaving one morning. As I stood in front of the mirror, thoughts started floating around in my head. Some were neutral; others were angry. While carefully manipulating the razor around my face and neck, I found myself dwelling on each disturbing thought for a time, adding commentary to each event, building them up, making them bigger. Each thought faded out as another appeared, leaving behind the irritable feelings of each passing thought on top of the other, to the point that I honestly could not recall which troubling thought was creating the discomfort in my body and throwing me off-balance.

Initially, I wanted the negative thoughts to go away. Paradoxically, this desire only gives them more power. Author Maria Nemeth, PhD, explains: "Trying to alter what your mind says forces you to dance with it, keep its rhythm, focus your attention on it. But as soon as you step out of the dance, your attention and energy are free to focus on the possibilities that surround you."[71] We can't stop our thoughts, and pushing them away only aggravates them and stirs up anxiety and fear. Gerry would assert, "Stop entertaining the thoughts!"

In the past, I would feed the negative thoughts. *The next time she is rude to me, I'm going to tell her off.* Old feelings would set in. An energy and heat inside me would rise up, emanating from somewhere underneath the thoughts and feelings, somewhere behind the story in my head. My first Buddhist teacher, David Nichtern, speaks often about this habitual pattern of building "story lines" and the emotional element underneath. In his article "How to Meditate Through Strong Emotions," David explains:

> *When it comes to experiencing strong emotions in our [meditation] practice, it can be helpful to notice that what we call emotions really has two major components. One is the "story line," which we do identify in our meditation practice as "thinking," and when we recognize it as such we are encouraged to let it go and return our awareness to our breathing and therefore to the present moment. The other component is actually energy that has a life beyond the "story line"—the energy and physical sensation of anger, passion, envy, pride, etc.*[72]

Thoughts arise and pass, or they drift into fantasy or planning, but they usually have little or no emotion attached to them. Storylines, on the other hand, or what we can call "feelings," have an emotional component. They are based on a personal narrative and are associated with past experiences, such as hurt, old wounds, trauma, cultural conditioning, and religious influences. In order to free ourselves from painful memories, conditioning, and influences (that don't serve us well), we can cultivate clarity and curtail the power of these negative storylines. When we sit in meditation and painful feelings appear, emotions like fear, anger, deep discomfort, and resistance might arise. Despite this, we must try to sit with the physical sensations of the emotions—that is, without the storyline. If we get distracted by a thought or a story starts unfolding, as David suggests, we return our awareness to our breathing. Then we go back to feeling the emotions and the energy they possess, feeling the sensations in our body, tuning in to the tone of the emotion, and resting there—the caveat being that if it gets too intense, we go back to the breath and slowly come out of the meditation.

I remember when all this became clear to me. While seated in meditation at home, I was focusing on my breath when thoughts of my former lover came to mind. We had broken up a year prior, but we were still friends. The storyline was strong. *Why did we break up? What happened?* I kept returning to my breath and the sensations in my body over and over again. Suddenly, out of the blue, tears started flowing. The thoughts kept intruding, but I stayed with the emotions. Then it hit me. I hadn't let go of her. I was holding onto her. I still had hope that we would be together again one day. Then and there, something shifted. The tears subsided. I felt liberated. Released. It was over. I had let her go.

Whatever emotion we're feeling, be it hurt, anger, fear, anxiety, frustration, or boredom, we sit with it and feel it. Instead of getting swept away by our emotions, we learn to regulate them by focusing on what they feel like in our bodies. We begin to decipher and distinguish the difference between what is a feeling (a painful memory, a storyline) and what is an emotion (a physical sensation). Indeed, on our meditation cushion, insights come to the forefront. *I'm still hold-*

ing onto that resentment I have toward my father. I need to forgive him. I need to let go of the pain. What was once in the background comes to the foreground.

In the long term, meditating allows us to become less bothered by disturbing thoughts, storylines, and emotions. They don't go away, necessarily; nevertheless, we begin to find comfort in the discomfort. The practice widens our comfort zone. On the cushion, we learn how to sit with the unwanted unease and uncertainty without panicking, without getting up to do something to distract ourselves, and without wishing them away. That said, the potency of the thoughts, feelings, and emotions do diminish, because our relationship with them changes. We let them be and learn to deal with them without getting easily rattled.

Gerry once told me a tale about a student who traveled far into the desert to meet his teacher, who was on a long spiritual retreat. As he drove his car closer to the teepee where his teacher was living, he witnessed whirling dervishes surrounding the teepee, creating a terrible racket. When he parked his car and made his way around them and into the teepee, he found his teacher in deep meditation. He waited quietly for an hour or so before his teacher slowly opened his eyes and greeted him. The student waited for the opportune time and asked his teacher, "How are you able to meditate with those whirling dervishes out there making so much noise?" His teacher replied, "I just let them whirl."

If you're a first-time meditator, try five minutes a day in the morning or before bed. A powerful calming meditation technique you can practice is soft belly breathing. Director of the Center for Mind-Body Medicine and clinical professor at Georgetown Medical School James Gordon explains:

Feel yourself relaxing with each exhalation, [deep breath] and know that when your belly is soft and relaxed, it helps to activate the vagus nerve. *Vagus means "wandering" in Latin, and this big nerve, which comes up from the abdomen, through the chest to the central nervous system in the brain, quiets the body and the mind. It's the antidote to the fight-or-flight response, the antidote to the stress response. And one branch of the vagus nerve, which is activated when you breathe slowly and deeply with your belly soft, allows us to connect more easily, more harmoniously, to other people. [It] activates centers in our cerebral cortex, which makes bonding easier. [deep breath][73]*

Soft Belly Breathing Meditation

Find a comfortable seated position, with your spine straight, either on the floor or in a chair. Use either a blanket or pillow to sit on. You can also prop your back up against the wall. Relax your shoulders, jaw, hands, and feet. Close your eyes or lower and soften your gaze. Breathe in through the nose and out through the mouth. Gently deepen the breath. Allow your belly to soften with each exhale. Silently say the word soft *when you inhale and* belly *when you exhale. Let this be your mantra:* soft *as you breathe in,* belly *as you breathe out. Breathe slowly and easily. When thoughts come, let them go. If you get lost in thought, return to the mantra. Continue for at least five minutes. Then slowly come back. If your eyes are closed, flutter your eyelids open. Move your fingers and toes. Stretch your arms and legs.[74]*

Finding Quiet

When we create a consistent meditation practice, a quiet comes. Gordon Hempton, author and founder of the One Square Inch of Silence Foundation, says that "Quiet is quieting."[75] And although he is referring to an external environment, it nonetheless applies to the internal. What's more, he says that in silence "anything can happen" and that silence "feeds our soul."[76] In the quiet, we gain clarity, tap into a deeper wisdom, experience inner peace, and hearken the voice of a Higher Power. In this state, we are guided, nourished, and uplifted.

In his article "Be Part of Something Bigger," Richard Miller, PhD, clinical psychologist and author, writes, "Meditation can help us get in touch with the universal life force that connects us all."[77] He explains how neuroscientific research has shown that meditation can help change the brain's wiring: "Meditation turns on and off a variety of pathways, or neural networks ... [that] can help you rewire your brain and gain access to those feelings associated with what yogis call shakti."[78] Miller describes shakti as the "universal life force."[79] He goes on to say that

Research published over the last several years in the journal Frontiers in Human Neuroscience *reveals that during meditation, your default network switches off. This is the network that enables you to locate yourself in time and space as an individual with a past, present, and future. While this network shuts down during meditation, three others—your attention, control, and present centered networks—remain switched on.*[80]

So, in effect, this network seems to shut down the ego. We lose our sense of self and we unself "feeling interconnected to the entire cosmos and at peace."[81] In that space, we are whole. And there, "Within each of us is unchanging equanimity, joy, and stillness, no matter what is happening in our lives."[82]

CHAPTER NINE

Magical Thinking

*Comfortable in our skin and in the world, we
can move freely with the rhythm of the universe,
receiving whatever it has to offer.*

We are all fascinated and moved by success stories along the lines of destiny, intention, and manifestation. There has been no shortage of popular self-help celebs and inspirational speakers sharing their extraordinary stories. In their books, television interviews, and college commencement speeches they encourage and motivate us to follow our dreams, embrace our uniqueness, and do whatever it takes, for however long it takes, to achieve our dreams and find happiness. These inspiring "dreams can come true" tales from celebrities and other luminaries give us hope. We are attracted to their confidence, exuberance, and promise of a happy life. And so we chase our dreams, searching for ways to manifest our visions into reality, thinking this will lead to happiness.

The celebrity sages state that "You can do anything you set your mind to" and that "If you put your mind to it, you can accomplish anything." They tell us that we all have a cosmic purpose and that our lives have infinite meaning. And although this may be a comfort to us, it is not evidence-based. It is magical thinking.

Magical thinking is the belief that thinking about something or wanting it to happen can make it happen. It's the belief that there are supernatural forces at work and that these forces can be manipulated in accordance to our *will*. Magical thinking never served me well. It just led to disappointment and endless despair. I learned on the sober path that "There is no magic in recovery. *We get what we work for.*"[83] That said, magical thinking cannot be proved or disproved, and my intention is to do neither. My objective is simply to scrutinize magical thinking, stoking the question—Is it serving you well?

For instance, dreaming about our fantasy car just moments before hearing a radio ad for it may be exciting if we think it is more than coincidence. Frequently seeing 11:11 on a clock or witnessing a double rainbow on our birthday may be comforting if we believe the universe or our lost loved ones are speaking to us. To be sure, rainbows can be spectacular. However, believing that they are signs or signals indicating that the spirits are alive and guiding us puts us in a wishful-thinking-like state and takes us out of the present moment experience. As I see it, adding meaning to external occurrences sidetracks us from the here and now and keeps us stuck in *self*, living as though things are happening *to* us.

When we add meaning to coincidences, trusting that they are messages assuring us that we are on track toward achieving our dreams and desires, we are forming expectations, building unrealistic hopes, and creating a personal reality outside of the laws of nature. When we look to the moon and stars for guidance, go to psychics for assurance, try to heal and grow spiritually through the assistance of crystals, create vision boards to manifest success, and give meaning to tea leaf messages and tarot cards, we are projecting our hopes and wishes onto them. We are subconsciously piecing happenings together to fit into our life puzzle or plan, mapping our wants and desires on to the universe rather than following the natural flow of the universe.

When we view the world from an egocentric perspective, believing that everything is happening to us, we vainly try to find meaning behind it all. When we are confronted with situations that are out of our control, we struggle and we suffer. We are uncomfortable living in an unstable world. Randomness keeps us on edge. We want answers. We want to make sense of it all. We feel powerless. And we cry, "Why is this happening to me?" We cannot see past our own egos. We cannot see that nothing is happening *to* us—it's just happening.

When we live with magical thinking, we are less likely to see the cause and effect, or what Buddhists call "causes and conditions." We look for cosmic meaning to grasp onto in lieu of reality. We shirk responsibility. We overlook the facts. We pass blame. When we feel off-balance, we consider what planets are in retrograde, overlooking that ten hours have passed since our last meal. We sidestep self-evaluation rather than seeing and admitting that eating fast food nearly every day for over twenty-five years may be responsible for our illness. Enchanted by mystery and imagination, we are blinded from what is real and obscured from the *now*. This is what living in a magical world brings on: myopia.

Reality is in the here and now, in the present moment; the rest is imagination. We need to face and experience what is real. Chögyam Trungpa reveals the truth of it:

> So the real experience, beyond the dream world, is the beauty and color and excitement of the real experience of now in everyday life. When we face things as they are, we give up the hope of something better. There will be no magic, because we cannot tell ourselves to get out of our depression. Depression and ignorance, the emotions, whatever we experience, are all real and contain tremendous truth. If we really want to learn and see the experience of the truth, we have to be where we are.[84]

The "real experience" of *now* cannot be found in the magical world. Spiritual gimmicks and New Age "feel-goodisms" cannot connect us to the divine. And so we must be careful not to cleverly disguise meditation gatherings and Sunday masses in spiritual wrappings to convince ourselves that we are living a spiritual life. Praying and singing in church, chanting until we are flying high at a kirtan event, or spending a month in Costa Rica drinking tea and practicing Yoga with like-minded people may be rejuvenating and replenishing, but until we acknowledge our powerlessness, surrender our will, and accept what is, freedom from suffering will never come to pass. We may think we are surrendering to a Divine Power by partaking in practices such as chanting, lighting incense, dancing with tinkle-bell anklets, summoning unicorns, praying, meditating, practicing asana, fasting, seeking healing through herbs, or going on wellness retreats, but we are not. Although rituals may be an act of self-discipline and self-sacrifice, they do not equate to the surrendering of the will. Devoid of surrendering, the prayers, the fasting, and the rituals are just forms of escape—escape from the fear, depression, and loneliness that inevitably return again and again. I heard someone say that spiritual retreats are like medicine. This may be true, but they are not the cure. At most, they are palliatives.

Magical thinking doesn't make us spiritual, just as believing in God doesn't make us religious. Spirituality and religiousness are actions. To live in the light, to free ourselves from fear and suffering, to experience grace, we have to do the spiritual work. Yes, these ritualistic disciplinary tools can work wonders, but only after we humble ourselves and accept what is. Until we do, these practices are just theater. They can look impressive and give us temporary relief and a feeling of transcendence, but once we go about our day, encountering daily life, the "love and light" we felt leaving a Yoga class or a kirtan event quickly fades away. As Trungpa says, we

can spend a great deal of money going on a religious "trip." But sooner or later, if a person is going to really connect with the teachings, there must be a return to the world. ... We may be sitting in meditation in our New York apartment, feeling very "high" and euphoric, very "spiritual." But then we get up and walk into the streets and someone steps on our toe and we have to deal with that.[85]

As attractive as the self-help promises of a good life and living out your dreams through intention, visualization, and manifestation might be, the spiritual work makes no such promise. The only promise the spiritual work makes is a life of inner peace, equanimity, and happiness. Whenever Vietnamese Buddhist monk, peace activist, and author Thich Nhat Hanh spoke about the "promises" of the spiritual work (or practice), it was evident he meant that happiness comes from within. Pursuing your dreams in and of itself is what is purposeful, no matter the outcome. This message is in no way magical.

The Spiritual Path

The risk of living in a dreamlike existence—looking for signs, waiting for messages, and hoping for happiness—is that we chance spending more time in the clouds and less time on the ground putting things into action. "If we see things as they are, then we do not have to interpret or analyze them further; we do not need to understand things by imposing spiritual experience or philosophical ideas upon them."[86] When we view and approach the spiritual practices pragmatically and not in a New Age "Dream it, believe it, and the universe will make it happen" manner, there is little left to chance, probability, or wishful thinking.

I'm not suggesting that we give up hope and stop following our dreams. Of course we can pursue our dreams, but we should leave the results or fruits of our work to the will of God (the laws of nature). Otherwise we submit to a waiting, an anticipation, a fear of never procuring our desires, and a fear of failure. Where there is hope and expectation, there is fear. And where there is fear, there is suffering.

"The word in Tibetan for hope is *rewa*; the word for fear is *dokpa*. More commonly, the word *re-dok* is used, which combines the two. Hope and fear is a feeling with two sides. As long as there's one, there's always the other."[87] Alternatively, when we focus on the task at hand without expectations, in the hopes that our purposeful pursuits will benefit others and hence bring meaning into our lives, we free ourselves from fear and suffering. This is spiritual living without magic.

When we surrender our will, see things as they are, we are more likely to be guided. Direction doesn't come to us through external occurrences and our five senses; it comes to us from within. Navigating through life pursuing outward signs is not the same as following your intuition and inner guidance. In fact, imposing our beliefs onto exterior happenings cuts us off from the inner world, which is why meditation is critical, for it clears the way. Without it, we see what we want to see. Meditation helps us to get out of our own way and break through whatever self-deception and denial exists within us. It peels away the layers of social, cultural, and religious conditioning, exposing true reality. It reveals our true selves and purpose. The great mystic Osho gets to the heart of it:

> *Meditation is fire—it burns your thoughts, your desires, your memories; it burns the past and the future. It burns your mind and the ego. It takes away all that you think that you are. It is a death and a rebirth, a crucifixion and a resurrection. You are born anew. You lose your old identity totally, and you attain to a new vision of life.*[88]

Yes, like a baptism or a psychic transformation. But as Trungpa points out, "This does not mean having an inspired mystical vision with archangels, cherubs, and sweet music playing. But things are seen as they *are*."[89] We awaken to reality, *as it is*, without wishful thinking, hoping, or expectations as Buddhists say.

No Hope, No Expectations

At first glance, the notion of living with no hope or expectations may seem bleak. On the contrary, relinquishing hope and expectations sets us free. It ultimately means living in the here and now without aching for things to be any better or even any different than they are. In the present moment, we are one with the universe and all things. This is our true nature and natural state of being—a state of wholeness, completeness, in which nothing is missing. Despite not being in an intimate romantic relationship, we can happily live alone without a nagging neediness and insatiable hunger. We can love and be of service to others without a desire for reciprocation. We can relax in our room and read a book, sit quietly and meditate, and speak openly with others and listen to their opinions without the urge to jump in and disagree. Comfortable in our skin and in the world, we can move freely with the rhythm of the universe, receiving whatever it has to offer.

Having no hope and no expectations frees us to take a leap of faith without an anxious concern of succeeding or not, and without being worried about the outcome. Whatever happens, we are accepting of it. We can breathe easy in the absence of a sense of urgency and a cutting craving for more. We can swim with the current of life, embrace the ebb and flow of the tide, and welcome whatever comes our way.

Having no hope doesn't mean we are hopeless; it simply means we are no longer desperately holding onto any hope. We are walking the path of least resistance. We are *being spiritual.* We are accepting whatever comes our way, however life turns out to be. Indian spiritual teacher and writer J. Krishnamurti is said to have put it this way: "Do you want to know my secret? You see, I don't mind what happens."[90]

To be clear, it's not as if we don't care what happens; it's that we are accepting of what happens, and we are no longer emotionally committed to outcomes. Yes, we still experience emotions; we just don't lose our sh*t over things because we aren't invested in fantasy or magical thinking. This is surrender and acceptance, not to be confused with capitulation or hopelessness. We can make plans, but they are open-ended. There is a curiosity, an openness, a sense of adventure, and a spontaneity to how we live. We are no longer trying to run the show. We are no longer desperately striving. We are practicing non-striving, like the Taoist concept of wu wei, which means "effortless action" or "actionless action." We are walking the path, but we are not *trying* to walk the path. We are opening up to grace but not chasing after it. We are doing the spiritual work, but with no expectation of an end result.

By all means, we must take action to get things done; "Faith without works is dead."[91] We cannot hope and expect the universe to magically bestow us with a better life. Hope doesn't get anything done. In fact, it's an obstruction. Hope hinders us from accomplishing meaningful change. Hope will not solve problems or make them go away. Problems will persist, unless we do something about them. We must act. As the saying goes, "Pray for potatoes, but pick up the hoe."

In his article "Beyond Hope," author and environmental activist Derrick Jensen writes,

When we stop hoping for external assistance, when we stop hoping that the awful situation we're in will somehow resolve itself, when we stop hoping the situation will somehow not get worse, then we are finally free—truly free—to honestly start working to resolve it. I would say that when hope dies, action begins.[92]

Everything said, we should set goals, pursue our dreams, and have faith; we shouldn't sit there to see what happens. But at the same time, we cannot fight the flow of the universe, nor can we run on self-will and force things in a self-help "manifest your dreams" fashion—not if we want to suffer less.

Again, Trungpa:

As long as you regard yourself or any part of your experience as the "dream come true," then you are involved in self-deception. Self-deception seems always to depend upon the dream world, because you would like to see what you have not yet seen, rather than what you are now seeing. You will not accept that whatever is here now is what is, nor are you willing to go on with the situation as it is. Thus, self-deception always manifests itself in terms of trying to create or re-create a dream world, the nostalgia of the dream experience. And the opposite of self-deception is just working with the facts of life.[93]

Letting go of our ideas of fate, destiny, cosmic purpose, and infinite meaning clears the way to follow our dreams with focus and fortitude. Surrendering our strong wants and desires unfolds a vibrant and adventurous new world right before our eyes. Once more, we can still attend to our dreams, but without a tight hold and constant craving and urgency. In this case, it won't matter whether our dreams come true or not, because we will have come to terms with what is. Or, put another way, we will come to accept that *our* game plan may not be in the cosmic cards.

No one knows if the universe has a plan for us. But if we choose the path of least resistance, we are more likely to recognize a plan if it does exist. By simply loosening our grip on *our* plan, we can create space for other possibilities to present themselves. American author and educator Parker J. Palmer says that it's more about "where it is my life is taking me rather than where I want to take my life."[94] Author and literature professor Joseph Campbell states it another way: "We must be willing to get rid of the life we've planned, so as to have the life that is waiting for us."[95]

To conclude, and to underline one more time: is magical thinking serving you well?

CHAPTER TEN

Realigning the Body and Mind

I routinely remind my students, "Trust your body—
our bodies are smarter than we are."

My body was a mess by the time I discovered Yoga. My chronic back pain and successive bouts of sciatica were slowly becoming unbearable. I had a year of sobriety under my belt and was ready to make another positive change in my life. As luck would have it, a gentleman from my therapy group recommended Yoga to me. I immediately took to it. At first I was unable to do much, which was not surprising, but what was strange was what happened at the end of class. Out of nowhere, during the final resting pose, tears flowed down my face. It seemed as if something deep down within me was signaling for my attention. I knew at that moment that I would continue taking classes.

It took a few years, but the classes relieved my back problems. Yoga also released unprocessed emotions that were deeply embedded in my tissues and bones and contributing to my overall bodily pain. Moreover, and without question, the breath work aided me in breaking a twenty-five-year-old cigarette smoking habit. Yoga naturally grew into an integral part of my sobriety and overall well-being (in addition to turning into my primary source of income as a Yoga instructor).

The word *yoga*, from the Sanskrit root *yuj*, means "to yoke." It is also interpreted as "union."[96] Yoga is a spiritual practice because it connects the body, mind, and spirit. It is an astounding methodology and science. In his influential and esteemed book *Light on Yoga*, Yoga master and author B. K. S. Iyengar writes, "Yoga is a timeless pragmatic science evolved over thousands of years dealing with the physical, moral, mental, and spiritual well-being of man as a whole."[97] He also writes that "Yoga is one of the six orthodox systems of Indian philosophy. It was ... systemized by Patanjali in his classical work, the *Yoga Sutras*, which consists of 185 terse aphorisms."[98] Iyengar goes on to mention the Bhagavad Gita and its explanation of the word *yoga*, but for the sake of time and space, I will abbreviate. (There are many books available on the subject.)

Through Yoga practice the body quiets. This, in turn, stills the mind of its fluctuations and focuses our attention. Yoga calms us. Whereas once we pounded the pavement, breathing short and shallow breaths and haphazardly handling situations in a heavy-handed manner, we now walk and talk with an effortlessness and ease. Moreover, we stay calm in the midst of conflict, expressing our thoughts and emotions more easily, hence circumventing preventable suffering.

In practical terms, we can learn and discover a great deal about ourselves simply through the asana (physical postures) practice. The postures and movement, in sync with the breath, aid us in being more present and focused. On the mat, we physically challenge ourselves, developing strength, flexibility, mobility, and confidence. Through regular practice, the mindful breathing and flowing movement matures into an active meditation that relaxes the body and mind, bringing about well-being. In fact, Yoga was developed as a way to prepare the body and mind to sit comfortably for long periods of time in meditation.[99] In light of this, whether in meditation or during the asana practice, one might witness "peak-experiences," as psychologist Abraham H. Maslow terms this occurrence:

In the peak-experience, such emotions as wonder, awe, reverence, humility, surrender, and even worship before the greatness of the experience are often reported. ... here in these experiences we discover a parallel to what has been considered to be the religious attitude toward death, i.e., humility or dignity before it, willingness to accept it, possibly even a happiness with it. In peak-experiences, the dichotomies, polarities, and conflicts of life tend to be transcended or resolved. ... The person himself tends to move toward fusion, integration, and unity and away from splitting, conflicts, and oppositions. ... There tends to be a loss, even though transient, of fear, anxiety, inhibition, of defense and control, of perplexity, confusion, conflict, of delay and restraint. The profound fear of disintegration, of insanity, of death, all tend to disappear for the moment. Perhaps this amounts to saying that fear disappears.[100]

I imagine we've all had peak experiences, which we could call a moment of transcendence or God-consciousness. Sometimes these moments happen spontaneously, like when witnessing a breathtaking sunset or waking up in the morning with a feeling of peace. Other times, this state of "fusion, integration, and unity" can be called up. Meditation, Yoga class, marathon running, mountain climbing, and skydiving are a few examples of how this experience can be evoked. That being said, the physical entryway to peak experiences will only gift us with transient ones. On the other hand, I believe Yoga is a systematic method that will lead us to a "peak life," as it were. The yogic principles can assist us in transcending fear and suffering. Specifically, every day can become a day of "wonder, awe, reverence, humility, surrender, and even worship before the greatness of the experience," as Maslow says.

The Wisdom of the Body

Just as with the recovery program, with the practice of Yoga, we get what we work for. Without a daily practice and discipline, we risk detaching from our bodies when the stresses of life overwhelm us, removing ourselves from our emotions, and losing touch with our breathing. In more extreme cases, those who witness or encounter physical or emotional trauma commonly disembody and disassociate. Yoga can help them reconnect, realign, and inhabit their bodies. By mindfully breathing and consciously moving, we establish (or reestablish) an intimate relationship with our body, tuning into its intelligence, signals, messages, and guidance. In other words, we em*body*. Dutch-American psychiatrist Bessel van der Kolk agrees:

> *Yoga ... fits very well with the increasing recognition that traumatized people cut off their relationship to their bodies. ... Emotions are expressed in things like heartbreak and gut-wrenching experience. So you feel things in your body. ... If people are in a constant state of heartbreak and gut-wrench, they do everything to shut down those feelings in their body. One way of doing it is taking drugs and alcohol, and the other thing is that you can just shut down your emotional awareness of your body. ... Yoga turned out to be a very wonderful method for traumatized people to activate exactly the ... areas of the brain, the areas of your mind that you need in order to regain ownership over yourself. ... Breathing, in particular, resets some critical brain areas that get very disturbed by trauma.[101]*

He further explains,

> *Western culture is astoundingly disembodied. ... We basically come from a post-alcoholic culture. People whose origins are in Northern Europe had only one way of treating distress: namely with a bottle of alcohol. Northern American culture continues with that notion. If you feel bad, take a swig or take a pill.[102]*

Most certainly, that's what I had done for years: I carried on with "that notion." I drank, used drugs, and was "astoundingly disembodied." I had no body awareness or relationship with my body. I lived in my head. I was out of touch with my emotions. Only during sex did I feel the sensations of my body and heartfelt emotions. That was one reason I obsessively sought it. Sex was like a religious experience, like heaven. Intimate relationships, on the other hand, were hell. For a person who didn't want to feel his emotions, who would "do everything to shut down those feelings," being in a romantic relationship was a place of torment. Outside of infatuation and lustful desire, I couldn't deal with the realness of a relationship. Simply put, once feelings like hurt, vulnerability, distrust, jealously, and disappointment blossomed, I would shut down. That was also why I got addicted to masturbation and pornography. Certainly, it was no substitute for a warm body, but it was removed, detached, and far less complicated.

My religious upbringing was another reason I disconnected from my body. Christianity, or more specifically, the Catholic community I was shrouded in, instructed me to reject my bodily desires. For certain, when I took on a pejorative attitude toward my body, a self-punishing attitude ensued. I squashed and attenuated my cravings. Unable to feel or identify my emotions, I got angry without realizing it. I'd get uneasy and not know why. My body's quiet, delicate, discriminating messages were inaudible.

Our body is intelligent. It knows there is a problem before we do—meaning, before our conscious minds do. It nudges us, giving us subtle signals that there is a problem on the horizon. Can we hear the whispering message? If not, eventually the message becomes loud and deafening in the form of a breakup, divorce, heart attack, or stroke. Indeed, our gut (the enteric nervous system, or as the sciences have nicknamed it, the "second brain") is smarter than we are, and it communicates with the brain in our head. Neuroscientist Richard Davidson says, "Our gut ... has enormous influence over our brain. To say that the mind is just in the brain ... just ignores the body."[103] And again, from the book *Buddha's Brain*: "What happens in your mind changes your brain … . And what happens in your brain changes your mind, since the brain and mind are a single, integrated system."[104] So in effect, if the body breaks down, the mind suffers. And if the mind miscarries, the body suffers. Suffice it to say, we need to nourish both the body and the mind.

The body is immeasurably influential. But sometimes we don't understand even its intense and visceral messages. For example, we may get a strong sense that we are being manipulated by someone, but because we have been culturally coaxed into relying more on our intellect than our gut, we distrust our intuition. We disbelieve and question our body's warnings. We think they're coming from our imagination, due to social conditioning, prejudices, and triggers from past events. There is a failure in communication. We can't distinguish between what is real and what is not.

When we lose touch with the wisdom of our bodies, we disinherit the ability to decipher between real fear and F.E.A.R. (false evidence appearing real).[105] Gavin de Becker, author of the book *The Gift of Fear*, offers up his wisdom and insights about this topic:

> *True fear will always be based on something in your presence, and will always be based on something you perceive. The signal comes from your perception, from your senses. Unwarranted fear will always be based upon memory. And so it's something you remember, something you recall, something you're worrying about, or something you're thinking about. But something based on your actual environment is a gift.*[106]

When a physical presence is threatening us, we get a gut feeling that we are in danger; we sense it. We were built to perceive fear. We have survived as a species because of this gift. It would be unwise, wasteful, and dangerous to ignore it. We need to rekindle our relationship with our body. Only then will this mechanism work maximally to our benefit.

In Yoga class, I tell my students, "Less thinking, more feeling." The physical practice of Yoga and mindful breathing help us embody and tune in to the wisdom and intelligence of our body. We learn to listen to and trust our body's messages. For example, when we are eating and our body says it's full, we put down the fork. When it tells us it's exhausted, we rest. I routinely remind my students, "Trust your body—our bodies are smarter than we are."

Similarly, on the mat, our thoughts can be a hindrance. *Why can't I do this? What's wrong with me? This is too difficult. I can't hold this pose.* In class, the inner monologue may shift outward: *Look at how well she backbends. I'll never be able to do that. What a show-off; he's distracting and ruining the class for everyone.* Our inner life reveals itself to us; our ego, pride, fears, judgments, and self-criticisms confront us. Yoga practice becomes an opportunity to look inside. We are forced to face our thoughts, feelings, and emotions on the mat. Our beauty and ugliness pin us down. These revelations about ourselves spill over into our daily lives so that we begin to notice our behaviors, our reactions, the behaviors of others, and the interplay more intelligibly. We are given an opportunity to confront the causes of our suffering and transform them into happiness and gratitude.

Our body/mind relationship can begin on the yoga mat. It is there that we learn to trust our body's discernment. One of the world's greatest minds, Friedrich Nietzsche, said, "There is more reason in thy body than in thy best wisdom."[107]

Many benefit by practicing yoga solely as a form of physical exercise. All the same, these practices have a way of revealing more to us. This was the case with me. What started as physical exercise slowly turned into a spiritual practice and a profession as a Yoga instructor. One could say I got to the spiritual through the physical.

CHAPTER ELEVEN

Anger

I can remember Gerry saying to me,
"Carl, there's a part of you that likes being angry."

Growing up I learned to never suppress my anger. I believed that if I held in my anger and kept it inside me, I would at some point explode in a fit of rage, or, worse, I would drop dead of a heart attack or get cancer. To my recollection, the unspoken understanding in my family and in the culture around me was to release your anger and let it out.[108] And I practiced it wholeheartedly. I got quite good at discharging my anger. It was the norm for me. Confrontation came easily. Going out of my way to give someone a piece of my mind for what I saw as an insult always felt justified. Those people deserved it. Whether they were rude, condescending, or patronizing, they got an earful.

If someone cut me off on the highway or was driving too slowly in the fast lane, they became a victim of my contentious horn-honking and middle-finger-waving. After all, they needed to be taught a lesson. More than that, I got a sense of satisfaction telling people off. It was cathartic (which was a popular term at that time). I rarely felt remorseful for releasing my anger on anyone. I thought it was the right thing to do. No one was going to treat me disrespectfully and get away with it. The cultural wisdom was that one should speak their mind, not be taken advantage of, not be a doormat, and not tolerate being disrespected. This mentality was mutually encouraged, supported, and validated among the people I grew up with. What's more, I witnessed it all around me, in the movies and on television. "He said what? If I were you, I'd be furious!"

I grew up in a rough town, and as a boy I had to be pretty tough to survive. I used to get into arguments and street fights on a weekly basis. Most of the kids I was exposed to were con artists, bullsh*t-ters, cheats, thieves, and risk-takers. They were always trying to get one over on you. I had to be cautious, watch my back, and be ready to swing at someone to defend myself whenever I walked down the street or hung out in the schoolyard. Standing up for yourself was the only way to establish (and maintain) your reputation as someone not easily reckoned with. Whether you won or lost a fight, what mattered most was that you never backed down or cowered before anyone. You had to fearlessly defend yourself, no matter how big, strong-looking, or crazy the other guy seemed to be. In fact, being crazy was advantageous. Crazy kept others from f*cking with you more than brawn did. Acting and looking like a psycho was a good skill to possess. I learned that if you were going to survive out there in the real world, you had to be bold and look a little bit deranged.

I remember hearing about therapeutic methods for releasing anger when I was in my late teens. Instead of suppressing anger, they suggested hitting pillows, buying a punching bag, taking up boxing, primal screaming in your car, or howling on your apartment rooftop. The scientific assertions were clear: Don't hold in your anger. People who did were the ones to be concerned with; they could detonate anywhere at any time. Sometimes these folks were reported on the evening news for "going postal." The sufferer of suppressed anger was like a time bomb ready to go off. When you were around them, their barely quelled anger was evident. You'd never know when they were going to erupt. They were unpredictable. When they did blow up, which was seldom, it was usually over something small. Their fits of rage were frightening and disturbing.

As for me, I was predictable; flying off the handle was expected. No one was ever surprised by my over-the-top explosive episodes. I was the guy they called hot-headed. Pretty much everyone pissed me off, and I made sure to tell them so. And although my anger was out of control and out of proportion at times, as an adult I was never physically threatening. Nevertheless, I imagine I was intimidating to some.

Before I started the spiritual work with Gerry, anger took up a large portion of my life. Looking back, it was the greatest source of my suffering. Over the slightest offense, I would transform from a calm state to an infuriated one in a matter of seconds. I had little self-restraint and would react aggressively. Yet there were other times when I would unknowingly turn my anger inward, suppressing it. When I did this, something strange would happen. It was much like Dr. Jekyll and Mr. Hyde. A dramatic shift would take place within me. A tingling sensation would permeate my body. For example, one evening I was driving to a dinner party with my spouse at the time. She said something that upset me. I got quiet and withdrawn. A rush of heat rode up my body and encapsulated me. I turned numb and quiet. I shut down emotionally and slipped into an immovable state, and a heavy feeling of detachment poured over me.

As soon as I parked the car I slumped in my seat. When I was in this state, I found physical proximity or closeness utterly repellent. I hated to be touched. (Granted, there were rare moments when being held lovingly, tightly, and apologetically would snap me out of it.) Regardless, whoever had to deal with the malevolent Mr. Hyde would usually have little interest in comforting him.

As I reclined in the seat of the car for a good amount of time, in a sort of catatonic state, I somehow conjured up the strength to go to the party. But only after much to-do and pleading from my spouse. Still, I remained aloof. I couldn't help myself. Of course, this made everyone at the party uncomfortable. But I didn't care; I was too emotionally fatigued to care. Besides, I was getting used to these frequent happenings, and I suppose the people who knew me were also growing accustomed to them as well. In this case, after a couple of hours had passed, I slowly returned to a relatively normal state. But that was unusual. More often than not, such a state would last days.

Seeking Help

Only after my first marriage came to an end did I finally seek help, which is how I ended up in psychotherapy. Talk therapy played an important role in my life. This method of self-inquiry and guidance was a vital step toward my healing and personal growth. I found a space to share my thoughts and feelings, a place where I was given an objective analysis of them and my experiences. In therapy I probed my past, which led to a partial understanding of why I suffered from anxiety, addiction, and depression. I unearthed feelings I had unknowingly buried that were sustaining my unsound behaviors. Undoubtedly, I am indebted to the therapists who have helped me.

It is also true that for me, therapy outlived its usefulness. It served its purpose. Not that I won't need it again in the future. But there comes a time when we must live life and stop analyzing it. In my experience, the therapeutic process turned into an ongoing habit of unceasingly overanalyzing every difficulty in my life. I wound up endlessly reliving my past, tirelessly mulling over my problems, and spending too much time in my head. I became a chronic complainer, dumping my gripes onto my therapist, retelling every disturbance and inconvenience that occurred during my week. "I got another parking ticket from a cop just looking to make his quota." "My wife won't give me a break; I work hard all week, and I deserve a few drinks to de-stress on the weekend."

The desire to vent is strong because it makes us feel better. It gives us a sense of satisfaction. Naturally, venting to a therapist every week seems helpful. Problem is, that sense of satisfaction is always short-lived. For certain, venting changes nothing; it only strengthens the habit of venting. We vent and our problems persist. The following week rolls around and we are filled with a new set of complaints (in addition to the many old ones) for our therapist's ear.

A significant number of us are taught that venting our frustrations and anger—"I need to get things off my chest"—is a positive method of de-stressing. On the contrary, venting keeps our anger and troubles alive and well. Reliving, retelling, and replaying our daily and on-going issues can make them bigger and worse. Venting is not what it's cracked up to be. Actually, it wouldn't be a stretch to say that *venting* is just a euphemism for *complaining*. More than that, venting is often just another way to avoid looking at ourselves. It keeps us too busy blaming others to be able to see our role in our hardships. We play the blame game to sidestep responsibility and accountability. Blaming, like venting, is, as Brené Brown puts it, "a way to discharge pain and discomfort,"[109] which changes nothing.

I used to vent quite often to Gerry, justifying my anger toward someone or some situation. After a few years of working with him, he stopped listening. He didn't want to hear it any longer. When I would vent, he would stop me dead in my tracks. "God's the answer; what's the question?" he would ask.

Frustrated, I would insist that he hear me out. I would tell him that I had every right to be upset because of this or that. He didn't want to hear it anymore. I would get angry at him. Sometimes I would hang up the phone on him. Other times he would do the same. In the past, he had been my sounding board. He was patient. He listened to me. But not any longer. "Carl! Carl! God's the answer; what's the question?" he would petition, interrupting me each time I started to unload on him.

It took a while, but I began to realize what he was doing. He was trying to get me to stop verbalizing, analyzing, and justifying every disturbance in my life. He wanted me to stop making a big deal out of everything. He knew that I was letting my ego get the best of me, that I was, as they say in AA, easing God out (EGO). He wanted me to stop venting and go to God. He wanted me "let go and let God," as the saying goes. I guess he knew I was ready to change.

Again, talk therapy is invaluable. It provides a safe environment to acknowledge and work through unprocessed feelings, unresolved issues, and trauma. But there comes a point when we must move on. Unfortunately, many of us get stuck, tirelessly going over the same mistakes and misfortunes. We still seek the love we never received from our parents, we resent our partner for cheating on us, and we feel that life has dealt us a bad hand. On occasion, on the couch, we may have an aha moment and a breakthrough of sorts, but at the end of the day nothing much changes. We return home, get annoyed at the kids, get angry watching the evening news, complain, and go to bed feeling dissatisfied with life.

Our problem is a habitual one—habits are enduringly engraved in our minds. Most of us are unaware of these patterns. Gerry referred to this as the "old tape." Something sets us off and the old tape starts running. For many of us, our reactions happen automatically; they precede our thoughts. Our partner tells us they are unhappy and we get angry. Someone calls us a hypocrite and we strike back. We can't seem to respond any differently. These habits are so embedded in our brains and bones that it's almost impossible to root them out.

Take another example, the cancer survivor. The experience changes their perspective on life. They were once cranky and cynical, but now, given a second chance, they realize life is precious and short. They no longer sweat the small stuff. Getting furious over not having hot water for a shower in the morning becomes quite trivial. But months go by and they get caught up in the hustle and bustle and stresses of life again. Suddenly they find themselves complaining, judging people harshly, and becoming cranky and angry again. That's because, as Gerry so often put it, "We have a built-in forgetter." Without discipline and vigilance, we can easily slip back into our old familiar ways.

Old habits are hard to break. These strong patterns of behavior are nourished by repetition. For certain, we must behave differently. Our thinking will not change our behaviors; only action will. As the saying goes, "If you always do what you've always done, you'll always get what you've always got." Plainly, our thinking will not solve our problems because our problem *is* our thinking. A quote often attributed to Albert Einstein illustrates this notion: "We cannot solve our problems with the same level of thinking that created them."

Usually, our issues begin at an early age. Our thinking takes a turn and slants toward the negative due to circumstances, environment, and sometimes bad biology. Typically, a trauma occurs that alters our view of the world. Psychotherapy can assist us in discovering when this trauma took place and how it affected us. And most importantly, as Judith Herman, author of the book *Trauma and Recovery*, writes, it can free us from being "imprisoned in the wordlessness of the trauma."[110] In therapy, when we learn that we are not alone, that others suffer in the same way, that there is a vocabulary for our experience, that we haven't lost our minds, that "traumatic syndromes are normal human responses to extreme circumstances,"[111] most of us find significant relief. Still, as I later found, healing and recovery take more than inquiry, discovery, confession, and analysis.

Beyond Thought

There are some things that can't be figured out through thought. Van der Kolk explains,

> *We have these two different parts of our brain, and they're really quite separate ... our animal brain [and] our rational brain .... These two are*

not all that connected to each other. And so, the more upset you are, you shut down your rational part of your brain. … Everybody can rationalize what they believe in and talk endlessly about why what they believe is the right thing to do, while your emotional responses are totally at variance with seemingly rational behaviors. We can talk till we're blue in the face, but if our primitive part of our brain perceives something in a particular way, it's almost impossible to talk ourselves out of it, which, of course, makes verbal psychotherapy also extremely difficult, because that part of the brain is so very hard to access.[112]

Van der Kolk, in describing the method of eye movement desensitization and reprocessing (EMDR), demonstrates how physical movement, not thought, can help rehabilitate our brains and restore our thinking:

It does not work through figuring things out and understanding things. But it activates some natural processes in the brain that helps you to integrate these past memories. … If you move your eyes from side to side [as instructed through the guidance of a professional] as you think about distressing memories … the memories lose their power.[113]

Supplementary to EMDR are the epigenetic studies being done by professor of psychiatry and neuroscience of trauma Rachel Yehuda. She says that when something traumatic happens to us, we tend to either say "I'm fine" or we lose it.

And really, what we have to do is give ourselves a little time after an adverse event … and just listen to our bodies and give ourselves the space to be quiet and to heal and to see, to ascertain what has been damaged and try to counteract that by putting ourselves in the most un-stressful, healing environment that we possibly can have, to counteract some of

that and promote a biological and molecular healing process that might
forestall some of the epigenetic and molecular changes.[114]

She also points out the importance of acknowledging our feelings, feeling them, and asking for help "instead of running to someone to give you a sleeping pill."[115]

Yehuda suggests psychotherapy as a treatment. And again, I concur, we can benefit immensely from the therapeutic process, whether it be for the treatment of trauma, depression, or for the difficult times that come up in our lives that we cannot seem to bear or overcome. But we are not just mental, cerebral beings with narratives. We are emotional, bodily beings as well, and we need to connect and nurture those aspects of ourselves. Unquestionably, our rational-thinking minds play an important role in our well-being, but if we are to alleviate our suffering, heal, and live serenely, we will need to tap into a deeper *knowing*. These words of wisdom from Osho explain what I mean:

Buddha never needed any psychotherapy for his sannyasins [ascetics and seekers of truth]; those people were innocent. But in these twenty-five centuries, people have lost their innocence, they have become too knowledgeable. People have lost their contact with existence. They have become uprooted. I am the first person who uses therapy, but whose interest is not therapy but meditation, just as it was with Chuang Tzu or Gautam Buddha. They never used therapy because there was no need. People were simply ready, and you could bring the rosebushes without clearing the ground. The ground was already clear. In these twenty-five centuries man has become so burdened with rubbish, so many wild weeds have grown in his being that I am using therapy just to clean the ground, take away the wild weeds, the roots, so the difference between the ancient man and the modern man is destroyed. The modern man has to be made as innocent as the ancient man, as simple, as natural. He has lost all these great qual-

ities. The therapist has to help him—but his work is only a preparation. It is not the end. The end part is going to be the meditation.[116]

Understanding Anger

My thickest "wild weeds," to use Osho's words, were anger and aggression. When I started to get into unself work more seriously, I can remember Gerry saying to me, "Carl, there's a part of you that likes being angry." Over time it became clear that he was right. What I also came to realize was how anger took me for an emotional roller-coaster ride. When I held onto anger (which was often), my perception grew distorted and I suffered. I turned blind, unreasonable, and irrational. And it didn't take long for me to go off the rails, and then there was no reaching me.

Gerry knew this about me. "Carl, you have to call me sooner, before you get deep in the sh*t. When you get angry, you need to contact me immediately so we can nip it in the bud. You have to call me right away next time, as soon as you get snagged, before the anger grows. You'll just have to ride it out now. There's nothing I can do for you. I can't reach you now." He knew me better than I knew myself.

Yes, when I was deep in the sh*t there was no talking to me. And more often than not this embittered state led to depression. And then I would feel nothing. No anger. No emotions. Nothing. Just numbness (which was ultimately what I sought in the end anyway). That was why I drank excessively and indulged in drugs all those years—I didn't want to feel my anger, hurt, and disappointments. I was accustomed to this state of nothingness. I was content feeling nothing. And although my drug of choice and constant companion was alcohol, I tried every elixir out there at the time, latching onto anything that would dull my pain and suffering and send me into a trancelike coma. I started with marijuana, which quickly led to pills and powder. I indulged in uppers like Christmas trees and black beauties, downers like quaaludes and Valium, and mescaline, LSD, psilocybin mushrooms, cocaine, heroin, and morphine. I snorted carpet cleaner and model airplane glue. I tried anything and everything. If someone handed me something, I snorted it, smoked it, or popped it without hesitation. By the time I was seventeen, I was getting high every day. My goal was simple: oblivion.

But now, sober and clean, there was no escaping my emotions, especially my anger. And when I got angry, I had a habit of holding onto it for days, sometimes weeks. A woman at a recovery meeting once said, "I know I have to let go of my anger toward my husband to find peace again, but I want to hold onto it a little longer." It sounds insane, and in a way it is. There is something safe and warm about wallowing in anger. We feel protected, powerful, and in control. And the reason for this, although usually unbeknownst to us, is that our animosity, indignation, and pride protect us from other more delicate, vulnerable emotions.

While doing the unself work, there was a time when I would let my anger sit there in the background. I'd let it simmer for as long as I could, enjoying its delicious quality. I knew I needed to let it go, but I wanted to stew in it for as long as possible. These were the games I played when I first got into the unself work. I tested things to see how far I could go and how much I could get away with, trying to hold onto some of my old self for as long as I could. However, I eventually came to realize that it wasn't worth the risk. More often than not, I would wind up in the sh*t, losing whatever progress I had made.

My father certainly had anger issues. As a boy I feared his explosives outbursts. He was a great man in many ways and I loved him dearly, but he had a bad temper. No doubt, I inherited his temper. Looking back at my childhood, my mother, maternal grandmother, and two older sisters were strong and smart. It was a matriarchal environment. And to protect the family unit and keep everything secure and in order, they kept things from the men. I guess the assumption was that men couldn't handle difficult situations well. They didn't want to upset us. It's not like they kept dark secrets; they kept matters like illness or hurt feelings from us. "We didn't tell you that Mom was in the hospital because we knew you would get worried. She's home now and she is fine. It was only dehydration. That's all." "Don't tell Dad that Aunt Pat hurt Mom's feelings." They wanted to "keep the peace," as they used to say. Apparently, the men in the family gave the women of the household a good reason to cover up challenging circumstances.

As for me, later in life, this became my reality with friends and lovers as well. "Don't tell Carl you lost the keys to the car; he'll flip out." "If Carl finds out you damaged the garage door, he'll go ballistic." My friends feared my overreactions. I was unapproachable. People hid things from me to avoid being harshly ridiculed and shamed. "What's wrong with you? Why would you do something so stupid?" They didn't trust me because they knew I was unable to handle situations rationally and reasonably. My track record showed that I would lose it over the smallest things. And if I discovered that they kept something from me, my reaction was far from understanding; it was stinging. "No excuses; you lied."

No question about it, lying is harmful; it breaks the trust between people. Just the same, with this new perspective, I see why my loved ones lied to me. My arrogance and sensitivity nudged them into compromising their own integrity. They hid the truth in order to avoid disdain, drama, rage, and humiliation. I kept everyone around me on edge, making it extremely difficult for them to be honest with me.

Working with Gerry, I came to see my role in all my troubles. "Well, who got the ball rolling?" Gerry would ask. Me, of course; I was the one who made it impossible for people to be open and honest with me. I was the cause of my problems. Gerry had me admit that to myself, him, and God.

It was hard to let go of my old self and all my flaws, but Gerry pushed me to keep working at it. I continued to practice restraint. When anger arose, I refrained from acting out. And more often than not, I would call Gerry and he would talk me down off the ledge. I'd turn my anger over to God. These were Gerry's instructions, and I followed them, which wasn't easy for an atheist. Nevertheless, I prayed a lot. I prayed for strength. I prayed so often that I developed a growing concern about it. One afternoon I was walking down the street silently talking to God. I thought I was going crazy. I called Gerry and expressed my concern. I told him that I was speaking to God day and night. He responded by saying, "And what's wrong with that?"

I worked with Gerry every day. He would tell me to turn my will over to God. I was to do God's will, not mine, praying: "Thy will, not mine, be done."[117] Gerry would say, "If it ain't good, it ain't God." My interpretation of that at the time was that if my thoughts, intentions, words, or actions were negative, they were coming from my will and not God's. Gerry was resolute: "God is good. If it's positive, it's coming from God. If it's negative, it's coming from the devil." I made Gerry's Christian belief and terminology work for me. When he would talk about God and the devil, I listened. Why would I question him and start a debate about whether God and the devil existed or not? After all, he was selflessly trying to save my life. I understood the truth behind his words. The devil was me, which is to say, my will and my ego. And as for God and His will? Well, I knew that God was not me.

Whenever I was in a somber state, uncertain, crawling out of my skin, Gerry would say, "You're not trusting God." He would quite often declare, "God is everything or He's nothing." Gerry was faithful about breaking my will. Whenever I was feeling off-balance and slipping into a negative state, he would shout, "I can't; He can; I think I'll let Him." Gerry would go on like a preacher. "Back when you were deep in the sh*t, the devil didn't have to worry about you. Now that you're getting closer to God, he's coming on strong. Stay close to God, because alone, you don't stand a chance against devil."

110

One day I cried, "Is God testing me?" "No," Gerry pronounced, as he proceeded to set me straight. "That's not God, that's the devil messing with ya. He's slick. He's always waiting in the wings for an opportunity to snag ya. Once you think you got him figured out, he'll find a new angle and blindside ya. You've got to tell the devil, 'Not today, devil; not today.'" It was as if I was being exorcised, or perhaps it was more like an emotional detoxing. No matter; it was clear the devil represented *self* and that God defined love and all that is good. Gerry's way of looking at it couldn't be more simple: positive equals God; negative equals devil.

But I was a complicated guy, and I needed something more specific and elaborate. So Gerry introduced me to the Four Absolutes.[118]

The Four Absolutes

1. Honesty
2. Purity
3. Unselfishness
4. Love

I was to use them as a checklist. In practical terms and in application, I used them to check my thinking and to make sure I took an unself-like course of action in any given situation (if action was necessary). I referred to this list in all my affairs. I asked myself, "Is what I'm thinking or about to say or about to do *honest, pure, unselfish, and loving*? If the answers did not meet the criteria of the Four Absolutes, it meant I was in self-will and not God's will. And so I'd refrain. Specifically, if what I was thinking (assuming I paused) was dishonest, impure, selfish, or unloving, I didn't speak or act. When I wrote a text or email in the heat of anger, I didn't hit send. I paused. I waited a few hours or until the next morning. I would read it over once I cooled down and gained some objectivity. When I did this, I was more likely to be thankful that I didn't send the message.

It's a simple strategy. We pause and check over the Four Absolutes. It sounds easy, but it is not. As I put this into practice, I began to realize how difficult it was to do God's will. But as Gerry insisted, "Change happens slowly." I had to keep in mind that I had been a particular way for a long time; how could I expect to change overnight? Moreover, we can't put a time frame on our progress, so we have to continue working at it for however long it takes. We must try to trust and have faith in the tools and techniques of the unself work. Change does come but never as quickly as we like. But when it does come, the Absolutes become a working part of our heart and mind.

CHAPTER TWELVE

Working with Aggression

Anger and aggression have a pernicious influence on us.
Over time, our reactive actions become habituated
and integrated into our bodies and minds.

Anger is a secondary emotion. Humiliation, frustration, disappointment, rejection, hurt, guilt, shame, regret, and jealousy (to name but a few) are the primary emotions that often lead to anger and aggression. I propose that there is also a sub-primary emotion underlying all emotions and responses, and that emotion is fear (see Chapter 15). For example, when one is rejected by their lover, fear sets in: "I'm not lovable. I'm destined to be alone." Of course, feelings of hurt, disappointment, and shame arise, and these feelings often lead to anger and bitterness. Yet fear, the underlying emotion, often goes unnoticed. Same goes for a threat, wherein we feel unsafe and vulnerable. Our natural response is anger, but it is fear that activates the fight-or-flight response, not anger. Anger is the emotional response and the energy we generate to help us fight or flee.

I didn't understand that anger is an emotion and aggression is an action. I didn't know there was a difference between them: meaning, anger and aggression. I got angry and, in turn, aggressively responded to whoever annoyed me. I thought there was only one way to express anger—furiously and forcefully. I didn't know that anger could be expressed in appropriate and productive ways. Moreover, I believed that my occasional loss of self-control and slamming of the door was the fault of my offender. I took no responsibility for what I saw as a justifiable action.

Anger is unavoidable. We cannot stop it from coming to the surface, nor should we. However, there are therapeutic ways to experience our anger, process it, and express it. Much to my surprise, I discovered that anger can be communicated constructively without aggression—although aggression isn't the only way we mishandle anger. There are those who repress their anger; they unconsciously hold down their anger, not letting themselves feel it. They become overwhelmed in difficult or hostile situations. They might shed tears, freeze, or shut down. They frequently think that they are fine, yet in reality they are numbed out and disembodied. They are detached from their emotions; they might display passive-aggressive behavior toward others but not know why. Others suppress their anger; they feel it and know it's there but consciously choose to stuff it down. Of course, we can't bury our anger and expect it not to localize somewhere. Whether it be toward our friends, family, children, pets, or in the form of a psychosomatic physical or mental illness, repressed or suppressed anger will always find a destination to reside in.

In a civilized society, fighting and reacting aggressively are harmful, provocative, unwise, and unhealthy. Conversely, fleeing is inappropriate, uncivil, and passive-aggressive. That said, anger is not the problem, per se. The problem is aggression, repression, and the suppression of anger. Getting angry is natural. Problems occur when we lash out, block our anger, or stuff it down. Developing an awareness of our strong habitual patterns of behavior and triggers is an important step toward understanding ourselves, breaking these habits, and gaining freedom from suffering. And of course, we must get more in touch with our emotions. If someone rejects us, we must get into the practice of residing in the fear, hurt, and arising anger; refraining from building a storyline; and resisting the urge to escape those uncomfortable, vulnerable emotions.

A Radical Change of View

Years before meeting Gerry, I discovered Buddhist philosophy. It turned my Western perspective of anger upside down. I was taken by it. I welcomed it. And I explored it and other Eastern philosophies with great curiosity and enthusiasm. Of most significance was something I heard the Dalai Lama say. He basically said this: Anger cannot be released like a hydraulic pressure system. Aggressively expressing anger will not relieve the sufferer of his anger; it will only create more anger. *What?* I thought. *How can this be? Getting the anger off my chest and out of my system, telling people off, letting them have it is fueling my anger?* This was unlike anything I ever heard. The idea was the antithesis of how I expressed and experienced anger. It stunned me. How odd. This strange man, this monk from a distant land, punctured my convictions in an instant.

All the same, this new information, this knowledge, which made sense to me, didn't change anything. I remained an angry, aggressive person. I didn't know how to let go of anger. I seemed incapable of it.

During my talk-therapy sessions, long before the recovery work, I remember realizing that I was dying a slow death due to my anger. It suddenly made sense to me that I was harming myself and causing my own suffering. I knew anger was toxic, poisonous, and destructive. Still, I got angry all the time. I wished for the rudeness of others to roll off me, but it would not. I could not rise above it. My anger was inescapable.

I discovered in therapy that forgiveness would relieve me of my suffering. Yet I was incapable of it. I tried, but I couldn't do it. I couldn't *just forgive* someone for wronging me or offending me. I didn't yet know the methods and tools that could help me. Only years later, while doing the recovery work with Gerry and digging more deeply into Buddhist methodologies, did I learn that change takes more than knowledge; it takes practice.

I learned in recovery that my problem was "lack of power."[119] Gerry explained it to me and would remind me often, "Carl, you need to get God-strong, not Carl-strong." Yes, I needed to go to God. I needed to surrender to a Power greater than myself. Gerry told me that my anger was blocking me from my Higher Power. And so we went deeper into the spiritual work of unselfing. Gerry convinced me, with solid evidence, that my problem was inflated ego due to low self-esteem. And because of this, my pride was easily bruised, so every curt remark angered me and every disagreement was an affront. Nothing rolled off me. Any perceived obstacle or offense slammed my ego. Naturally, I compensated for my low self-esteem by being aggressive. In a disagreement or conflict, I combatively confronted my offender. I demanded respect.

I had little to fall back on other than respect. Unknowingly, I felt inferior. And subsequently, any disagreement or hint of condescension from someone would enrage me. Anger and aggression were my defense. And it kept me from seeing the reality that underneath the surface, behind the anger, lived a hypersensitive guy who didn't like himself.

When we possess an enormous ego we tend to take everything personally. We react angrily when things don't go our way. We feel like a victim of what is happening around us. We don't feel in control of situations, people, and our environment. And so we go to anger because it gives us a feeling of power. It can become our default mechanism, a hardwired response. We cannot help ourselves; the urge is too strong. We are overpowered by it, and consequently we lose our self-control.

There's a reason why spiritual practices emphasize the importance of undoing the ego. When our ego is running the show, we take everything to heart. A careless remark from someone can set us off. "Who do they think they are, saying that to me? I don't let anyone speak to me that way and get away with it!" Our ego often gets the best of us.

You might be thinking, *Ego or no ego, why shouldn't I get upset when someone is rude to me?* Well, I used to feel the same way. Once I got deep into the unself work, whenever I tried to express my upset about someone or something, Gerry would interrupt me and ask why I was angry. I would response by saying, "What do you mean? Why shouldn't I be angry? The person was condescending." And again he would ask me, "Okay, but why are *you* angry?" The question would frustrate me to no end, until one day he asked me to read this:

It is a spiritual axiom that every time we are disturbed, no matter what the cause, there is something wrong with us.[120]

I told him the axiom was ludicrous. "If someone insults me and I get angry, I am to blame? There is something wrong with me?" I rejected the notion wholeheartedly. But Gerry carried on about it. And so, as with every suggestion of his, I eventually started to apply it. The instruction was to stop blaming others for my upsets, anger, and reactions. I was to turn things around and look at myself. "Why am *I* disturbed?" "Why am *I* agitated?" "Why am I so easily bothered?" "Is there a reason why I'm this way?" "Was it what I witnessed growing up?" "Were my parents this way?" "Did they handle conflict badly?" I was to practice self-restraint. I was to look at the situation objectively and honestly. If I was wrong, I had to admit it. If they were wrong, I had to forgive them.

Most of us were never given instructions about how to deal with anger. Likely our parents weren't given the tools either. And so, like them, we were left to our own devices, with no understanding, no guidance, and no skills. All we had was our default mechanism to fall back on; our hardwired survival, primal instincts; and inadequate role models we witnessed at home, in school, on television, and in movie theaters.

After getting into the recovery work, many things came to light. I was likely this way my whole life. I would pout and sulk as a boy, and this carried over into my adulthood. I realized how I was blaming others for all my heartaches, holding them responsible for all my upsets, disturbances, and hurt feelings. In effect, I had been unable to see outside my victim mentality. Indeed, denial blinded me from seeing the role I played in each situation, thereby preventing me from growing emotionally and depriving me from having healthy and functional relationships.

Anger and aggression have a pernicious influence on us. Over time, our reactive actions become habituated and integrated into our bodies and minds, so much so that we no longer see them. As Gerry often said, "Denial is a powerful thing." And denial has no bounds. I could now see that whenever I had felt hurt, I would sullenly shoot daggers at people and punish them with silent scorn, as if to teach them a lesson—the lesson being, "Don't hurt me and think you can get away with it." It became alarmingly apparent that I had done this to most everyone in my life. I was harsh, cold, and fiercely unforgiving.

As the walls of denial came down, it became clear how much damage I had done over the years. So much so, that I began beating myself up about it. But Gerry was clear: "We not only have to forgive others, we have to forgive ourselves as well." If I was to grow and heal, I had to let go of my past mistakes. If I was to repair the damage I caused, I had to trust the process of unselfing. Yes, some of the damage I caused was irreparable, but I had to believe that my past experiences could benefit others. I couldn't wallow in self-pity and remorse, which would just trade one form of suffering for another. I had to forgive myself. And I had to continue the spiritual work.

The Way of the Bodhisattva

Under the umbrella of Buddhism, it was American-born Tibetan Buddhist nun Pema Chödrön who most penetratingly spoke to me. Her books and talks shifted my view of anger and aggression dramatically, and her perspective is most profoundly presented in a dharma talk in which she dissects the eighth-century Indian Buddhist monk Shantideva's first fifty-one verses of *The Way of the Bodhisattva*.[121] The verses and her commentary struck home for me in a resonant way. Among the verses, the following questions were asked and answered, which Chödrön interpreted and elaborated on:

1. What purpose does anger serve?
2. Does anger help us get what we want?
3. Does anger make us feel good?

I got honest about each question. I lived with them for quite some time. What purpose does anger serve? Unquestionably, anger serves me well if I am in physical danger or in a life-threatening situation or crisis, helping me find focus and strength. But other than that, how else does anger serve me? At this point I knew my anger, aggression, and resentments were killing me. In the recovery rooms I witnessed many men and women who would repeatedly pick up the drink every few months only to return to the rooms counting days again. And whenever their backstory was revealed, it was apparent anger took them out. That said, I was one of the lucky ones; I got angry often, but I never picked up. Nevertheless, my anger and aggression ruined most relationships in my life and nearly ravaged me. In my sobriety

I discovered that I didn't need to drink to destroy my life. My anger reigned in the damage department; it didn't need any assistance. Without a doubt, anger didn't serve me well.

Does anger help me get what I want? Well, as Gerry and I went through the spiritual work of unselfing, the walls of denial came crashing down and the truth revealed itself to me: I had lost several jobs, plenty of career opportunities, and countless friendships due to my anger and aggressive behavior. At this stage of the game, it was apparent how kindness and patience would have gotten me what I wanted rather than self-righteous, angry demands. I once heard Nhat Hanh say something to the effect that people really only listen to love letters. I remember the basic idea being that if we treat our opponent with respect and loving-kindness (a term Buddhists use), if we write a love letter to our local politician rather than an angry one, we will more likely be heard and manifest our intention. Simply put, if you want something from someone, you're more likely to get it by being calm and kind rather than screaming in their face. So, no doubt, anger does not help me get what I want.

The third and last question: does anger make me feel good? This is a tricky question. Anger may not feel good in our bodies, but when it's released, boy, it feels good. The satisfaction I would experience when verbally striking out at someone was addictive. It was a high. Although, as with any high, it was short-lived and it came with a hefty price. For one, my explosive eruptions toward others would leave me with a dreadful emotional hangover. For two, my fits of rage would often culminate in regret and embarrassment. And last, my aggressive behavior would harm others, including my loved ones. I always thought that releasing my anger on the person who caused it would relieve me of my anger, but I was wrong. The Dalai Lama was right: aggressively expressing anger will not relieve the sufferer of their anger; it will only create more anger. So, the answer to this question is no, anger doesn't make me feel good.

Being Vigilant

I needed to learn how to express my anger in a more restorative manner if I was to suffer less. Gerry's message was clear and in line with Buddhist teachings—vigilance is vital. We have to be watchful of our thoughts, words, and actions and take mental notes of our negative patterns of behavior. They are automatic, habitual, and often undetectable at first. But if we are mindful, we will notice them. As I observed my own conduct more closely, I recognized the strong pull to follow the same old patterns of behavior. I would react with aggression whenever a sharp comment was thrown at me. I'd even get angry at myself for missing an opportunity to respond angrily to an affront, due to being caught off-guard.

Identifying my character flaws was not easy, but my new awareness led the way. I recognized that I was on guard all the time, and it kept me on edge and in a state of constant anxiety. Additionally, I had to let go of any resentments I had as a result of past incendiary remarks or criticisms. I had to forgive my offenders. I couldn't continue living the same way, not with a clear conscience, anyway.

Whenever I slipped up and lashed out, I had to make amends without justifying, clarifying, or downplaying my wrongs. I had to forgive those who mistreated me. I had to stop taking inventory of others by pointing out their mistakes and misdoings; I had to instead focus on my wrongs and making things right. Gerry instructed me to take a daily inventory, noting each time I got bothered and the reasons why. This was what I practiced. Although I failed again and again, I continued to work at it. Whenever a disturbance arose, I went to the spiritual axiom and asked myself, "Why am I disturbed?"

I was quite astounded at how often I got upset. At first, these upsets seemed small and insignificant, but it soon became apparent how these trivial annoyances kept me endlessly uneasy and unhappy.

Gerry opened my eyes to see that much of our suffering is not hidden somewhere in the dark recesses of our minds; no, the causes of our suffering are right in front of us, impeding us from enjoying life. They are not the big events, per se; they are the small and often unnoticeable things that happen throughout our day. They don't seem like anything to be concerned with most of the time. But these seemingly insignificant occurrences are the cause of much of our suffering. They are powerful and insidious, and they hinder us from being happy.

So, why did I get angry all too often? Well, I was avoiding distressing feelings like disappointment and hurt. Hurt makes us feel vulnerable, and that can be frightening. Anger is our protective shield against feelings of vulnerability. Of course, fear is present, underneath the anger. We fear that we will lose control of the situation, fear that we will be abandoned. Some fear they will break down in tears. As long as we continue to hold onto our anger when it comes, we will never be able to acknowledge our fears and feel our hurt. What's more, we will never be able to work through our disappointments and pain. "If we do not transform our pain, we will always transmit it."[122] Namely, our unprocessed pain will manifest itself into passive-aggressive or aggressive behaviors and without question, endless suffering.

In hindsight, I understand that hurt and fear were foreign to me. They were sensations in my body that I didn't have a name for, that I never let myself feel. They were far too uncomfortable. And so when I felt them, I would immediately jump to anger. It was my go-to. I was in my comfort zone when I was angry. That was my safe place. I felt strong and unafraid.

Admitting our feelings to the one who hurt us is a bold gesture. I remember when I first started helping others in recovery, I was fascinated to find that some married men would rather climb Mount Everest than apologize. I'd told one guy, "Buy your wife flowers and say you're sorry." He just couldn't do it. I realized there was an inequality in his relationship. He didn't want to relinquish his power. He was protecting his position. But unbeknownst to him, he was shutting his wife out.

For sure, it's safer to protect ourselves in a quarrel. By putting down our guard we fear opening ourselves up to more hurt and to future hurt. We fear looking weak. But the truth is, no one worth knowing is going to take advantage of the situation and add salt to the wound while we are exposing our hearts.

This is where surrender comes in, helping us resist retaliation and revenge toward someone who hurt us, admitting our mistakes, being the first to say "I'm sorry" (whether right or wrong), and forgiving others. For some of us, these actions might be relatively easy to do. For me, they were nearly impossible. As I got deeper into the spiritual work, I remember several times sleeping on the couch after a fight with my partner. I would lie there, knowing damn well that if I got up and went back to bed and apologized (regardless of who was at fault), I would be graced and released from my anger and suffering. I knew this because I had done it before. Still, it remained a struggle. I would sit up on the couch and then lie back down in a huff. I would stand up and then sit back down, resisting, fighting my ego and pride, wanting to stay angry, wanting her to come to me on the sofa and apologize. But, as if she (and God as well) knew that this was my lesson, she would seldom come to me. I had to be the one to get up and slip into bed, hold her, and say "I'm sorry." Sure enough, though, every time I did, without fail, my trapped, tense body, wrapped up and bound in shackles, would immediately be released from the suffocating weight of anger. The pain would float away as if the devil himself were being exorcized from my flesh by the good Lord Almighty. Grace would then soothe me, and the warmth of my partner would ease me into a soundful sleep. As sure as the sun will rise, whenever I say "I'm sorry," the spell breaks, and I am free again.

Public speaker and spiritual guru Gaur Gopal Das offers this sutra, or precept: "When you say a [*sic*] sorry, it doesn't mean that you are wrong. It just means that you value the person and the relationship more than being right."[123] No doubt, these actions are self-sacrificing. Of course, there are no guarantees that self-sacrifice and surrender will free us from emotional, psychological, physical, and spiritual suffering—this is where faith and a trust in *what is* comes into play.

Most, if not all, of the spiritual practices are clear that vulnerability, honesty, humbleness, and heart—essentially unselfing—lead us on the path to happiness and freedom. It takes courage to forgive or admit our wrongs, but the more we open up our hearts, the stronger and more courageous we become. In the end, if we are to be free from suffering, we must let go of our anger and forgive. For we must "lay down [our] weapons and armor and proceed onward. ... As [Irish novelist and clergy] Laurence Sterne said: 'Only the brave know how to forgive.'"[124]

Of course, anger will still arise, and so will the desire to react or retaliate. We need to pay attention, pause, and resist the urge to fall back on the same old tricks. Only then do we stand a chance of doing something different. The suggestion is to breathe, stay in the moment, and refrain from fueling the anger. In an interview with Bill Moyers, Chödrön speaks about this strong pull and getting "hooked":

Hooked is an interesting quality to me. ... I mean, not only has something evoked a response in me but it's going to be difficult for me to let go. Anger is like that for sure. Prejudice is like that. Critical mindedness is like that. You don't want to let go. There's something delicious about finding fault with something. And that can be including finding fault with one's self, you know? So that's what I mean by hooked. ... the image of a fish and the hook and it has this juicy worm on it and you know the consequences aren't going to be good. But you cannot resist. And one of the main things we're addicted to is escalating aggression.[125]

Similarly, Gerry used to say to me, "Don't take the bait!"

As time rolled on, I dug deeper into the unself work. I began to see changes. Notably, the rudeness of others was starting to roll off me. This was nothing short of miraculous. I was sure something else was at work here, something beyond me and my abilities, ostensibly a Power greater than myself. I was gaining the ability and strength to surrender my *self*, my wants, and my strong desire to react angrily. I remember thinking, *I like this. And I want more of it.* It was a glimpse of something outside of my experience. And it was a clear indication that the inside work was transforming me.

CHAPTER THIRTEEN

Radical Change

Making amends got me to see that whenever my
feelings were hurt, my go-to was anger and retaliation.

In relation to anger, I saw three phases of transformation take place over the course of a couple of years. The first was gaining an ability to pause, refrain, and walk away from a provoking situation. I still got angry, but I was able to resist the strong desire to aggressively respond—albeit I would step away grumbling under my breath and grinding my teeth. The second phase (which came months later) was the faculty to pause, refrain, walk away, *and* let go of the anger fairly quickly. And the third (which took many more months) was the strength to pause, refrain, walk away, and let go of the anger *immediately*, letting my feelings toward the person who provoked me quickly transform from outrage to compassion. These happenings were unlike anything I had ever experienced. And they carry on as long as I continually surrender my *self* to a Higher Power.

Some time back, while attending a school concert, a fellow parent I was seated next to offered me an opportunity to practice the practice. Throughout the performance my neighbor kept checking his social media account every three minutes. It was clear he wasn't checking his texts for an urgent message; he was scrolling through his feed. I felt my anger and annoyance of this inconsiderate distraction growing within me. So I began to talk to myself. I started reasoning with myself. *What's going on here? Is this my ego? Is this me wanting him to behave as I think he should? Is this me wanting him to play by the same rules as the rest of us? Okay, Carl, calm down. This is not such a big deal. You're happy to be here enjoying the show. Why ruin it for you and everyone else? Let it go. Take your focus off his phone and enjoy the show. It's actually not even that distracting. His screen light is dimmed.* I continued this sort of problem-solving self-talk and proceeded to talk my *self* down. I was able to ease my anger, calm myself, and drop into discernment rather than judgment. *This guy is addicted to his phone. He literally can't resist checking it. He can't seem to relax. Poor guy. Thank you, God, that I don't have that struggle.*

That wasn't the end of it, though. No, I had to forgo fanning the flames of anger after the incident as well—which is to say, I had to resist the urge to vent about it to others afterward. "You're not going to believe what this guy was doing during the concert!" When we hold onto an agitation, verbalizing it again and again throughout the day or week, we are feeding it and keeping it alive. That said, if our frustration and anger must be expressed to someone, we should reserve our emission to one person, like our therapist, sponsor, mentor, or partner. Even so, we must let go of the heat behind it, and we mustn't go on about it.

As I continued following Gerry's instructions and applying Buddhist teachings to my daily interactions, transformative changes took place within me that seemed beyond my doing. I sensed a mysterious aspect to these milestones, as if something outside my *self* was the cause. Was it a Higher Power or an inner intelligence? Whatever it was, I couldn't will it, and I was powerless over controlling it. All I could do was surrender to it. When I did, I was frequently guided and gifted with a power I otherwise lacked. Whenever a difficult situation came about with my partner, an intelligent, honest, and nonaggressive response or nonresponse came forth. The appropriate words or action emerged, as if involuntarily. Rather than reacting aggressively or suppressing my anger, which was my normal reflex, I remained calm. Words flowed from my mouth like fresh water. "What's wrong? Why did you say that to me?" Letting down my guard, I acquired strength. Being vulnerable, I tapped into a tender place. My urge to angrily snap transformed into heartfelt words such as "That hurt me." I realized that restraint and not placing my partner on the defensive, and sometimes even walking away and giving her space, would more often than not defuse the situation. And surprisingly, whether immediately or sometime later, it would lead to her apologizing and telling me what was wrong.

The Power of the Pause

Pausing is critical. Whenever I pause, I stand a greater chance of handling a provocative situation in a more rational and understanding way. Chödrön speaks a great deal about anger and the practice of pausing. Chödrön suggests,

> If you wait and don't fuel the rage with your thoughts, you can be very honest about the fact that you long for revenge; nevertheless, you keep interrupting the torturous story line [going on in your head] and stay with the underlying vulnerability ... relaxing with that restless, hot energy—knowing that it's the only way to find peace for ourselves or the world.[126]

She also writes,

> So what do we usually do? We do exactly what is going to escalate the aggression and the suffering. We strike out; we hit back. Something hurts our feelings, and initially there is some softness there—if you're fast, you can catch it—but usually you don't even realize there is any softness. You

find yourself in the middle of a hot, noisy, pulsating, wanting-to-just-get-even-with-someone state of mind: it has a very hard quality to it. With your words or your actions, in order to escape the pain of aggression, you create more aggression and pain.[127]

When we get hit with that penetrating rude remark, there is hurt. We feel attacked. But if we pause, refrain, and watch the rising anger, we can avoid doing damage to ourselves and others: "If you're fast, you can catch it." If we "keep interrupting the torturous story line," we stand a chance of not reacting in a regrettable way. Osho also offers helpful insights and tools in working with anger and aggression:

Remember, we pour our energy into anger, then only does it become vital. It has no energy of its own; it depends on our cooperation. In watching, the cooperation is broken; you are no more supporting it. It will be there, for a few moments, a few minutes, and then it will be gone. Finding no roots in you, finding you unavailable, seeing that you are far away, a watcher on the hills, it will dissipate, it will disappear. And that disappearance is beautiful. That disappearance is a great experience.[128]

Watching is vital. But this is difficult at first, nearly impossible. The self wants to fight back; the pull is strong. But with consistent practice, we can do this and turn less reactive and more able to recognize our anger and refrain from acting out. This is how we change our automatic, habitual responses. However, at the start, we feel powerless to let go of anger. All we can do is our part—pause, refrain, breathe, not fan the flames of aggression, surrender our will, and turn our anger over to our Higher Power.

Another Buddhist teaching that radically shifted my understanding of anger and reshaped my practice comes from Nhat Hanh. He writes,

In his Discourse on Mindful Breathing, the Buddha taught, "Breathing in, I recognize my feeling. Breathing out, I calm my feeling." If you practice this, not only will your feeling be calmed down but the energy of mindfulness will also help you see into the nature and roots of your anger. ... [When we practice mindful breathing,] first, we recognize the presence of, for example, anger in us, and we allow it to be. We do not try to suppress or express it. We just bring the energy of mindfulness to our anger and allow our mindfulness to take care of it the way a mother holds her baby when it begins to cry. We ... care for our anger, to calm it down.[129]

How wonderful is that? Instead of causing harm to ourselves and others with our anger, we take care of it—like a loving mother would take care of her child.

Anger is not the enemy; it is there to tell us something, to help us. Nhat Hanh's teaching suggests we develop a healthy relationship with our anger in which we care for it and calm it down instead of fueling it and aggravating it. We hold it, cradle it, and cultivate patience, compassion, and a gratitude for it. And "we must continue, continue, continue," as Gerry often said. But woefully, we can be hard ourselves, which is why I welcome the little reminders of my progress.

One day I was driving with my thirteen-year-old daughter on a two-way street. I made a three-point turn. There was a box truck in front of me, so I anticipated oncoming traffic on the other side. I paused, but an approaching car slammed on the brakes, thinking I was going to proceed. A brawny young man jumped out of the car. Standing a safe distance away, he started screaming at me. As I opened my window to explain, I paused and just sat there observing his out-of-control, hostile tirade. He went on cursing me. I suppose out of frustration with my nonresponse, he jumped back into his car and drove off, but only after a few final expletives. I reflected for a moment and turned to see if my daughter was okay. Thankfully, she was. I said to her, "I used to be just like that man, but thank God I'm not any longer." She smiled, and I carefully completed my turn and drove away. Reflecting on the incident, I remembered how unhappy I had been living that way. But it was the only way I knew how to be. I felt only empathy toward the young man, no anger or ill will. Gratitude poured over me. The unself work was helping me see this aggressive person as a struggling person, like me.

Passion vs. Compassion

Strong feelings can lead to intense emotions and sharp words. We can get easily drawn into heated debates because of our "passion" for a particular cause. "I'm not angry. I'm just very passionate about this campaign." There is a fine line we often walk between passion and anger that puts us at risk of losing our heads. In the past, whenever I was accused of being loud, assertive, and aggressive during a discussion, I would often respond by saying, "I am just being passionate." Years later, after the inside work, I realized this was untrue. Passion, outside of love and sexual desire, is emotional, "as distinguished from reason."[130] I did get heated and angry; my emotions did rise high. I became irrational and judged others harshly. And further, I most certainly suffered from post-polemic emotional hangovers.

Aggression often hides under the attitude of "being passionate," but there are differences between feeling passionate and being passionate. When Martin Luther King Jr. gave his "I Have a Dream" speech, he delivered his message passionately, yet he did so without anger or aggression toward his opponents. He spoke strongly from his heart. Trungpa writes,

If you are passionate, you want to get something quickly to satisfy your desire. When there is no desire to satisfy yourself, there is no aggression or

speed. The absence of aggression … is the definition of dharma. Dharma is defined as "dispassion" or "passionlessness," and passionlessness implies absence of aggression.[131]

I would go so far as to say that passion without aggression is not only passionlessness, it's compassion. That is, "consciousness of others' distress together with a desire to alleviate it."[132] In light of this, MLK's speech wasn't passionate at all in the sense of being "intense, driving, or overmastering feeling or conviction"[133]; no, it was compassionate. And through compassion, MLK could be steadfast in his stance against injustice and inequality while treating his opponents with respect and dignity.

These distinctions are important to point out. What was extraordinary about MLK's presence, actions, and words (which we also witness in his "I've Been to the Mountaintop" speech) was the absence of anger, bitterness, resentment, retaliation, profanity, self-importance, self-righteousness, and indignation. He demonstrated nothing but compassion, love, understanding, and a deep trust and faith in God. What's more, and just as extraordinary, he knew that his enemies were suffering too. Nhat Hanh, who worked with MLK, knew this as well: "We suffer and we do violence to each other just because we cannot understand each other's suffering. We believe that we are the only people who suffer. We think that the other side does not suffer. We believe that they only enjoy our suffering."[134] I concur: where there is anger and hate, everyone suffers.

Contrary to popular belief, we absolutely can aim to achieve what we want and stand up for what is right without aggression. This is true no matter how great the cause or injustice may be, and MLK was proof of that, without question. We can disagree with people and say no to injustice without feeling furious and full of rage. In fact, it would be wise to let go of righteous anger. Intolerance and indignation offend people and place them on the defensive, whereas tolerance and understanding gift us with a better chance of communicating our cause or argument. In truth, any struggle for change can be done successfully with decency and honor.

Sadly, in the past, I thought this type of restraint was too compromising and weak. "Hey, I'm just being honest, straightforward, and saying it as I see it." I believed that this posture was powerful, assertive, and self-reliant—but it is not. It is impolite, unrefined, and aggressive. Moreover, I believed that I was being honest. But honesty need not be abusive, crude, vulgar, insulting, selfish, or careless. No, honesty, that is, thoughtful honesty, is tied to sincerity, integrity, high principles, and right-mindedness.

I learned that by pausing, stepping back, and reflecting on the situation, I can access sincerity, integrity, and the like. But if I push on with anger and frustration, I ultimately diminish my usefulness, lose my peace, and suffer. I stand a much better chance of accomplishing my goals by approaching a situation with self-control and stability. I am more likely to be heard if I am rational and levelheaded. What's more, if I remain calm, compassionate, and understanding, I am less likely to demonize my opponent and more likely to hear and respect my opposition's stance and, at the very least, come to an agreeable compromise.

Loving Speech

Loving speech comes from the Buddhist tradition. It's a mindful way of speaking (and listening) that centers on compassion, kindness, and understanding as a way to avert suffering.

Generally speaking, loving speech is an all-or-nothing deal—which is to say, we can't compartmentalize it. We can't be aggressive in our business dealings by day and be happy, loving, and relaxed with friends by night. We can't be angry at our boss at work and go home feeling calm and peaceful. Our anger will spill over in some shape or form—we will be impatient with our kids, snap at our partner, and want to eat dinner alone in our office upstairs because we "have work to do."

To practice loving speech, I need to maintain what Buddhists call equanimity, which means the highs are not too high and the lows are not too low. My teacher David would say, "Not too tight and not too loose." In this middle place, we keep a steady mind. If we find ourselves getting drawn into the heat of a debate, we step back, pause, and take a few deep breaths.

One of my Yoga teachers suggested I use the Four Gates of Speech as a checklist. Although often attributed to the Buddhist and Sufi traditions, a similar framework can be found in other spiritual practices and religions.[135] It turned out to be another helpful tool that I added to my spiritual arsenal. We can use it as a checklist, preempting our choice of words.

The Four Gates of Speech

1. Is it truthful?
2. Is it necessary to say?
3. Is it the appropriate time?
4. Is it a kind thing to say?

If the answer to any of them is no, I pause, especially in the heat of anger and frustration. Remember, we must practice self-restraint. When we are driving in slow-moving traffic, before slamming on the car horn, we pause and ask ourselves, *Is it necessary?* If we're having an interaction with someone and emotions heighten, we pause and try to calm down by using mindful breathing. On social media, don't comment on a post in the heat of anger. Or, as previously mentioned, when writing a text or email, don't hit the *send* button when upset and out of sorts. Put it aside for a few hours or a day. After a time, when the anger has dissipated, look at it. You will likely rewrite it; "You will find that the person who finishes the letter is not the same person who began it. Peace, understanding, and compassion have transformed you. ... That is the practice of loving speech."[136]

On the other side of the coin, loving speech starts with how we speak to ourselves. What is our inner voice saying? Is it self-judging? Severe? How do we speak about ourselves in the presence of others? Are we critical of ourselves? If we don't speak kindly to and about ourselves, we will likely be unable to speak kindly to others.

When we are in a negative state of mind, our thoughts and feelings, fueled by intense emotions, can turn exaggerated. We must take into account that most thoughts and emotions come and go and have little or no meaning. They carry no weight and have no substance unless we attach a storyline to them. Suffice it to say, we must develop a skillful mind (which derives from the practice of mindfulness and loving speech); otherwise, whenever our emotions run high, we risk firing away at ourselves or the nearest target.

In keeping with loving speech, by and large, most arbitrary thoughts are not necessary to share. Contrary to the mentality of some who proclaim, "I want you to be honest with me. I want to know what you're thinking and feeling," some thoughts and feelings are private. Don't fall for such intrusive requests. Just because you don't share every single thought or feeling with a friend or lover doesn't mean you are not being honest. Why unload every random rumination, feeling, emotion, dream, or fantasy on someone? Most of the time they are just meaningless. Sometimes they are irrational. And most of them don't represent us and who we are as a person. Most of the time they are just passing thoughts and feelings driven by electrical signals that run through our brains and body, over which we have no control.

Making Amends

What came next was by far the most arduous part of unselfing. Gerry indicated that it was time to make a list of the people I had harmed, those I'd have to make amends to. Of course, he explained, there would be amends I could never make directly, either because the person was dead, their whereabouts were unknown, or contacting them would harm them or others. Once we decided who fell into this category, I made amends to those people in spirit. I wrote down every apology on paper and read them out loud in front of Gerry and in the presence of God. As I finished each one, I tore up the paper, asking for forgiveness and for the strength to forgive myself.

When it was determined that contacting a person to make an amends would be in the best interests of all parties, I reached out to them for their approval. In the case of person-to-person amends, Gerry gave me specific instructions. He informed me that this would be more than a simple apology. "Saying 'I'm sorry' was something we did many times over the years; what good did it do?" He explained that saying "Sorry" to someone only relieves us of our remorse and shame; it does little or nothing for the other person.

He instructed me on how to go about making proper amends. I was to ask three questions, the first question being, "How did my inappropriate behavior affect you?" Gerry advised me to let the person speak, keep quiet, listen, and not interrupt them: "No *ifs*, *ands*, *buts*, or excuses explaining why you did this and why you did that." When they finished, I was to ask them the next question: "Did you leave anything out?" If they did, I was to let them tell me without interruption. When they were done, I was to ask the last question: "How can I make it up to you?" Typically this approach of making amends is usually well-received. As Gerry told me, "People usually answer by saying, 'You already did make it up to me just now.'" All the same, there are no guarantees. And so, as Gerry advised, whatever response you receive from the person, accept it with humility.

It's plain to see that this method of making amends is far more powerful than simply saying "Sorry." It gives the other person the opportunity to explain how we affected them and how they felt and feel. It's much more gratifying for them to have a chance to express themselves and to have their say than to receive a simple apology. Indeed, humbling ourselves in order to bring healing to those we have harmed takes courage. Humbleness—or, more broadly, humility—is a principle found in most religious and spiritual practices. And humility is a by-product of unselfing. Pastor and author Rick Warren says, "True humility is not thinking less of yourself; it is thinking of yourself less."[137] Humility is a virtue, not to be confused with humiliation, which is demeaning and undignified.

To be sure, making amends in this manner was a lesson in listening and humility. It was strange sitting silently and listening. In a few cases, it was shocking to hear their side of the story. Their experience of what happened was always quite different from mine. Moreover, in listening to their narrative, I learned a great deal about myself.

I will never forget one particular time I made amends over the phone. It was with an old friend who I'd cut out of my life. I emailed her, and she agreed to speak to me. When I asked her, "How did my inappropriate behavior affect you?" She said, "You were dear to me. I had no idea why you ended our relationship and why you were so angry with me. I was deeply hurt and heartbroken. I thought we were good friends. I loved you." It struck me hard. I was shocked. I had had no idea what harm I had done. More than that, I assumed she knew why I'd gotten angry, cold, and distant. *Didn't she realize that what she said to me was stinging? Didn't she?* Well, of course not! How could she know? I never told her. I didn't tell her why I was hurt and angry. I never gave her a chance. I was too emotionally immature to have a heart-to-heart. And I was too sensitive to see it for what it really was—nothing. In other words, what she had said to me years ago wasn't a big deal, and it certainly wasn't worth ending our relationship over. Needless to say, she didn't know that my ego was so easily bruised by the slightest offhand remark. She didn't know that I was a pouty, spiteful child. And she didn't know that I was distrustful of people. And in a sense, neither did I.

I proceeded to asked her the following two questions: "Did you leave anything out?" and "How can I make it up to you?" She said no and that my amends were appreciated. I sincerely apologized and thanked her for sharing her side of the story. Once we hung up, I fell to my knees and wept. I had treated many of my friends and lovers the same way over the years. I greatly wronged and injured the people who loved me. I was unforgiving and incapable of simply saying, "That hurt me." My anger and pride had ruined many meaningful relationships. For the first time since working with Gerry, I genuinely asked God for forgiveness.

Making amends got me to see that whenever my feelings were hurt, my go-to was anger and retaliation. My attitude had been to stand hard and protected. Gerry had suffered from the same symptoms. On occasion he referred to himself as King Baby Gerry.[a] He pointed this out and helped me see the same insecure, sulking, spiteful, childish shortcomings in me. His depth and wisdom woke me up to the harsh reality and truth of it—I never grew up. I didn't just act like a child; I was a child. And a bratty, ornery one at that.

I had never outgrown the behaviors I developed as a child. I suppose my mother, who loved me unconditionally, tolerated my behavior far longer than she should have, which is likely the reason why it continued into my adulthood: it worked! That is, with my mother. In the grown-up world, I found that love was conditional. And so, King

---

a. Only later did I come upon Sigmund Freud's phrase "His Majesty the Baby" regarding narcissism and infantile omnipotence. See Freud's *On Narcissism*.

Baby Carl didn't always get his way. Many close relationships had ended over my juvenile behavior.

I woke up and grew up as a result of the unself work. I had to learn how to express my anger and hurt appropriately, without causing unnecessary suffering to myself or anyone else.

Making amends to those we've harmed, when appropriate, is a necessary component for our growth and healing. Likewise, it is also vital that we forgive ourselves for the harm we have done. We can't beat ourselves up. We must watch out for self-pity, for it can lead to depression and hopelessness. Of course, it is normal to feel self-pity now and again, but we mustn't wallow in it.

With Gerry's help, my view of the world began to change. I wouldn't say I'd woken up entirely quite yet, but the walls of ignorance and denial turned porous. (I use the word *ignorance* as Buddhists define it: not as stupid but as unaware, unawakened, unwise, and misperceiving true reality.) That said, Gerry was clear there was more work to be done.

CHAPTER FOURTEEN

Working with Resentments

But the choice is ours—we can look more honestly at ourselves,
or we can choose to plug away at shielding ourselves from
people and situations we find difficult.

Long before the recovery work, I didn't know what resentments were, nor did I know the kind of nefarious impact they were having on me. As I worked with Gerry, I realized I had resentments galore. I came to know them well. Resentments don't go away—not on their own accord, at least. But by developing a regular routine of prayer, meditation, and compassion practice, we can rid ourselves of our resentments.

When we hold onto anger and let it build up inside us, when we strongly savor our dislikes, when we demonize a person or group, we construct resentments. We inherit triggers, in which, for example, something suddenly reminds us of a person who insulted us, and our anger comes to a boil. An incident that may have happened months ago or even years ago turns us sour in an instant. We go back in time, reliving the incident that angered us, and strong emotions arise as if time hasn't passed. More drastically, the negative feelings that are born out of resentments can turn destructive and corrosive, leading us into dangerous territory.

Does the thought or mention of a particular person or past situation stir up anger, spite, and hostility in you? Do you wish certain people ill will? These are resentments. And when we persistently hold onto them, we turn bitter and suffer. When we replay, relive, and reexperience an injustice, offense, or unfair treatment, it becomes deep-seated. "Time heals all wounds" does not apply here. Some of us carry around resentments for years. And often we feel justified in doing so. After all, we were wronged. Unfortunately, we don't see how we are cutting our nose off to spite our face. We are living with the toxicity of bitterness while our "enemy" goes about their life.

Resentments can lead to thoughts of retaliation. We may never act on our vindictive thoughts, but they are damaging just the same. They elicit suffering. So we must rid ourselves of them if we want to live a sane, happy, and peaceful life.

To start, we need to be willing to work with our resentments. An unwillingness to do so will have cancerous consequences. Our readiness rides on how strongly the ego resists, which is why it is wise to surrender the self. Of course, if a relationship or situation caused an emotional or psychological trauma, getting outside help would be wise. A trauma brought about by abuse, loss, death, or involvement in or witnessing of a life-threatening situation can linger for years unless we get professional help. That being said, in addition to professional services, spiritual help is necessary.

There is immense immunity in letting go of our resentments. But letting go is not easy. Freeing ourselves from them can be difficult, but we must. This advice from a prominent clergy aided me in the past, and it continues to, as long as I am willing. It's referred to as the Resentment Prayer:

If you have resentment you want to be free of, if you will pray for the person or the thing that you resent, you will be free. If you will ask in prayer for everything you want for yourself to be given to them, you will be free. Ask for their health, their prosperity, their happiness, and you will be free. Even when you don't really want it for them and your prayers are only words and you don't mean it, go ahead and do it anyway. Do it every day for two weeks, and you will find you have come to mean it and to want it for them, and you will realize that where you used to feel bitterness and resentment and hatred, you now feel compassionate understanding and love.[138]

As Bill Wilson, the author of Alcoholics Anonymous anticipated, you might be thinking, *Whoa, this is a tall order!* Well,

Do not be discouraged. No one among us has been able to maintain anything like perfect adherence to these principles. We are not saints. The point is, that we are willing to grow along spiritual lines. The principles we have set down are guides to progress. We claim spiritual progress rather than spiritual perfection.[139]

And so we practice unselfing. We just do it, whether we want to or not; we go through the motions. We fake it till we make it.

We mustn't fall victim to the false feelings of power and indignation that anger and resentment offer us; they will only harm us in the end. We needn't forget the wrongdoing, but we need to be willing to forgive. The notion "Forgiving doesn't mean forgetting" only works when we truly forgive and wish our wrongdoer well. This way, when the thought of the person who wronged us comes to mind, we will remain equanimous. When we faithfully forgive someone or something, our thoughts, storylines, and emotions shift from evoking fear and anger to bringing about understanding and compassion—or, at the very least, neutrality. When we start to see people as sick and suffering beings, we free ourselves from the poisonous anger, fear, and underlying unease that perniciously percolate in our body. When we genuinely think of our offenders without anger or hatred, we suffer less, turn happier, and experience a great freedom.

Compassion

Cultivating compassion toward our enemies can be found in many traditions, such as Buddhism and Hinduism. If you are holding onto a resentment toward someone who bullied you or shamed you, take a few minutes to sit quietly and breath mindfully. Call them to mind. Imagine them as an innocent child. Something must have happened in their life that caused them suffering. Someone must have broken them so that they had little chance of doing anything other than what they did to you. Try to soften your heart.

Taking a more compassionate view of others will help shift our perspective. I learned in the rooms of recovery that when

> *we begin to see that all people, including ourselves, are to some extent emotionally ill as well as frequently wrong, and then we approach true tolerance and see what real love for our fellows actually means. It will become more and more evident as we go forward that it is pointless to become angry, or to get hurt by people who, like us, are suffering.*[140]

Unequivocally, this new perspective will not arrive by thought alone; we must take action. We must display compassion. We must demonstrate tolerance and understanding toward our fellow sufferers. Surely, this stance was contrary to my instincts, or should I say, my go-tos. It was unlike the defensive stance I was accustomed to taking. "Don't be easily hurt." "Don't be taken advantage of." "Never show them fear or shed tears." "Never let them get the best of you." "One-up them if you must." Yes, this stance is quite the opposite. It is one of strength, courage, and forgiveness. It's a spiritual stance. And it will be difficult and awkward at the start. It certainly was for me. It didn't feel genuine at all. But Gerry told me to hang in there and stay on track. "It goes from the head to the heart," as he put it. That is to say, we understand it first in our head, then someday we begin to feel it in our heart. When we act and live compassionately, we *become* it and it *becomes* us.

The Opportunity to Practice

Buddhists believe that all of us are inherently compassionate and good, that underneath the fear and anger there is goodness. Fascinatingly, they do not view people who wrong others as bad but rather as having unskilled minds. The Buddhist practice is one of compassion and non-judgment. Even those who physically harm others are not looked at as evil; they are instead viewed as unawakened. I remember hearing the Dalai Lama expressing this idea: The people we find difficult, who test our patience, who anger us, should not be viewed as enemies or as people we should avoid; they should be viewed as gifts we can learn from. Which is to say, gifts that give us the opportunity to practice patience and tolerance.

Of course! How else can we practice these principles? How else can we grow into understanding and compassionate human beings? Certainly, these virtues cannot be acquired from books. We can't practice patience, tolerance, compassion, and understanding alone in our room. Nor can we unself by diverting difficult people and situations. No, on the contrary, this is how we avoid the practice of patience: by sidestepping provocative people. So, the suggestion is simple, albeit considerably hard to put into practice: Instead of developing a dislike toward the people who get under our skin, practice gratitude; they are gifts!

It's easy to shun the people who agitate us and proclaim, "I only want positive people in my life: those who nourish me, support me, and are kind to me." We can carry on repeatedly sounding off the "No bad vibes; good vibes only" mantra, but the truth is, these provocateurs are difficult because they challenge us. They penetrate our painful past and they touch a sensitive and hurtful experience we have yet to work through. By avoiding them, we avoid the arduous healing process. Unquestionably, removing ourselves from those who make us uncomfortable is just another way we bypass addressing our own untreated and unprocessed emotional and psychological issues. (This is sometimes referred to as "spiritual bypassing" in Yogic and Buddhist communities.[141])

"Problematic" people make us uncomfortable because they act as a mirror, reflecting back our own unwillingness to look deeply inside ourselves. They reveal to us places that are still sore and broken. They bring out the judgmental part of us, our anger, insecurities, sensitivities, and doubts. They force us to look at an aspect of ourselves we'd rather not see. "I just don't like him; he rubs me the wrong way. His views and opinions are backward. He stresses me out and makes me angry."

There is a fine line between walking away from flawed friends and alienating oneself. We must be careful not to flippantly label someone toxic just because they disagree with us. The bottom line is that it's impossible to completely shake off difficult people and situations anyway. We can try and try, but we will never succeed. Even if we were to isolate ourselves from others and live alone in a cave on a remote island, we would still have to face threats and challenges. Caves get cold, dark, and damp, and beautiful islands get infested with biting insects. And as for our inner demons—they follow us wherever we go.

It would be better to face our fears and learn how to be less bothered by people and demanding developments. But the choice is ours—we can look more honestly at ourselves, or we can choose to plug away at shielding ourselves from people and situations we find difficult. I'm reminded of a Buddhist story I once heard about a prince who aspired to gather up enough hide leather to cover the streets of the city. Each time he left his castle he would burn his feet on the hot pavement, cut them on shards of glass, or stub his toes on uneven surfaces. In short, realizing that there wasn't enough hide leather to be found to cover the city streets, he had an epiphany: wear leather shoes.[142]

The Sick and Suffering

It will take time to develop patience, tolerance, and understanding. So, until that time comes, we may need to stop seeing certain people, avoid particular places, and abstain from doing things because we lack the skills and strength to be able to handle the people and situations that provoke us. At the beginning of our journey we practice limiting our triggers, not as a way to avoid life but with the intention of later easing back into it with a new attitude.

If we have a drinking problem, it's best to not go to bars and parties where there will be drinking. If we are a spendthrift, we should cut up all of our credit cards or let our partner hide them. While living with heartbreak, it would be in our interests to stop listening to sad songs and love songs, to withdraw from looking at our ex-lover's social media page, and refrain from viewing romantic movies. If we often and easily get angry and rush to judgment on social media, we may need to unfollow friends who provoke us, or at least hide their posts. Whatever we have to do, we do it until we get mentally, emotionally, and spiritually fit.

Having said that, mentally fit or not, we may have to end some relationships that have become toxic. In that case, it may be best to confide in a friend or therapist about it; another point of view can be invaluable. And although it may be easy to place blame, we shouldn't get hung up on who is right or wrong. We all play a part in our relationships. We must look at our role both curiously and honestly. If we do part ways, we do so with compassion, not anger; with understanding, not intolerance; with good wishes, not ill will; and with forgiveness and tenderness. If anger or thoughts of retaliation come, we go to love. As for the people who cut us out of their lives (for whatever reason known or unknown to us), we wish them well; we wish them love and happiness.

We can take our cue from the great Nelson Mandela. After spending twenty-seven years in prison for standing up for freedom and resisting oppression, the activist, revolutionary, and eventual president of South Africa was quoted saying, "As I walked out the door toward the gate that would lead to my freedom, I knew if I didn't leave my bitterness and hatred behind, I'd still be in prison."[143] The Christian teaching to "Love thy enemy" is apropos; in the Bible, Jesus says, "But I say unto you, Love your enemies, bless them that curse you, do good to them that hate you, and pray for them which despitefully use you, and persecute you."[144]

Eventually, I began to see difficult people not only as gifts but as sick and suffering, too, just like me, or how I used to be. That's not to say that I'm immune to building resentments and getting sick again. No, I must remain vigilant. As the old saying goes, "There, but for the grace of God, go I." Meaning, I was once a suffering soul, but because of God's grace, I am no longer a sick man. And so it seems that as long as I stay on the path of surrender and unselfing in all my affairs, grace will abound.

But what is grace? What is this experience? Is it God's benevolence toward the unworthy, as the Christians believe? Well, supposing that God *just is*, neither benevolent nor malicious, how can it be grace? Could it simply be good fortune, then? Well, my gut tells me grace is more than an alignment of the stars, a confluence of elements, and being at the right place at the right time. Grace is higher than good fortune or luck. Grace is holy, like a church Mass, like a Bach cantata, like a Beethoven symphony. Grace is transformative; good luck is not.

Perhaps grace is a reservoir of energy, a fountain of love that the spiritual path leads the thirsty to drink from. For certain, I don't take it for granted. For although we can sip from its stream, we cannot contain it. Indeed, I am humbled by it and grateful for it. In fact, when I experience grace, humility comes quite naturally and gratitude overwhelms me. More than that, humbling myself to grace not only feels right, it seems to make it expand and flow, drawing me nearer to its depth and power. No doubt, when I bow to it, I feel its presence—a Power greater than myself, who I choose to call God. I experience what feels like benevolence. Because unlike luck or good fortune, grace feels like love. For sure, grace releases me; it washes away my guilt and shame, whereupon I am born anew.

When Resentments Reappear

Sometimes an old resentment will come back to visit us, either out of the blue or triggered by something. We might think nothing of it, but if we don't act quickly, it will get bigger. An old resentment (or a new one, for that matter) may seem weak and insignificant at first, but it will weave in and around our mind and overcome us before we know it. For instance, a few years ago, while lying in bed at night, I caught myself thinking about a past incident. It was a situation I wish I had handled differently. It happened three years prior, but there I was replaying the scenario in my head, rewinding it, and imagining ways I could have handled it better. I laid there in the dark beating myself up for not having responded more shrewdly. I fantasized and rehearsed similar possible scenarios in my mind, preparing myself as to how I would retort with a more satisfying comeback if given a similar opportunity again. Within seconds my scalp was sweating, the old feelings reemerged, and my peace slipped away. Suffice it to say, this type of thinking is detrimental to our well-being. We mustn't entertain negative thoughts and storylines. We have to let them go quickly, and the Resentment Prayer can aid us.

It's easy to get frustrated and angry at the reappearance of resentments. We desire them gone. But we are powerless over them. We cannot will them away, just as we cannot erase our past. It's a losing battle. No, we have to surrender our will and accept our resentments. We can't destroy them. Indeed, we need to give up the fight on the grounds that there is no war to win or enemies to conquer anyway. We are practicing compassion, which applies not only to our outer life but to our inner life as well. We are making friends with ourself, our resentments, our past, our fears, and our anger. We must; otherwise, we are going to do great harm to ourselves; "if a person dwells obsessively on the inner warfare, he or she can do as much damage to the brain as a lifetime of alcoholism or drugs."[145]

By changing our relationship and outlook, we are less likely to develop resentments in the future. I once heard a wonderful Buddhist story that captures this idea; it went something like this:

Long ago, an emperor went on a brief journey for the day. Shortly after leaving, an ugly, smelly, and angry monster approached his castle. The guards were so frightened that they let him in. His odor was stifling, and his language was foul. The monster seated himself on the emperor's throne. The guards realized their mistake and attempted to chase him away. They shouted at him and threatened him. At each abusive word and threat thrown by the guards the monster grew bigger, smellier, uglier, and his words become more alarming. This continued on, and the guards became more hateful and the monster grew bigger and bigger. When the emperor returned, he witnessed the guards screaming and violently throwing objects at the monster who was seated on his throne. To the guards' surprise, the emperor apologized for the rude and hostile behavior, welcomed the monster, and offered him food and drink. With each act of generosity and kindness, the monster shrank smaller, grew quieter, and became less angry, until he got so small that he disappeared.[146]

Outside of the Resentment Prayer, we can also rid ourself of our resentments by practicing *Metta* meditation, a Buddhist practice that translates to "loving-kindness." In this practice, we send loving wishes to all beings, including our enemies.

Loving-Kindness Meditation

Begin by finding a comfortable seat either on the floor or in a chair. With an upright spine, breath naturally and close your eyes. Focus on your breath for a minute or two. Now visualize a light from the universe entering through the crown of your head, going down your spinal cord to the base of your spine. See it grow and expand and extend to all the cells in your body. See it begin to direct itself to your heart. Repeat the following slogan three times silently to yourself, sending yourself good wishes.

May I be happy.
May I be healthy.
May I be free from suffering.
May I live with ease.

Now bring to mind a close friend, someone you care for and love, like your parent, partner, or child. Picture them in your mind and feel their presence. Envision the light coming from your heart extending out to their heart. See the light pulsating and growing brighter and bigger. Send them good wishes. Repeat the following slogan three times, directing it toward them.

May you be happy.
May you be healthy.

May you be free from suffering.
May you live with ease.

Call to mind someone you like yet don't have strong feelings toward—someone neutral. This could be a neighbor you say good morning to, or the mailman, or the friendly cashier at the market. Visualize them. Let the light from your heart expand and extend out to their heart. Send them good wishes, repeating the following slogan three times.

May you be happy.
May you be healthy.
May you be free from suffering.
May you live with ease.

Now call to mind someone you are angry or resentful toward, a person you find difficult, a person you are holding a grudge against. See them in your mind. Relax your body. Let your light grow. Extend your light to them. Let it enter their heart. Stay with them. See them. Send them the same good wishes you sent to yourself and the others, repeating the following slogan three times.

May you be happy.
May you be healthy.
May you be free from suffering.
May you live with ease.

Now bring to mind all these people. See yourself with them together in a room. Send your light to all of them. Then send your light to all the sick and suffering in the world. Let your light shine brightly. Slowly come back, taking a few deep breaths in through the nose and out through the mouth. Open your eyes and stretch your legs. Take this light with you as you go about your day.

CHAPTER FIFTEEN

Fear and Working with Fear

*Fear had been a stranger to me, lurking in the basement
and hiding in the shadows. It was an unsettling
feeling in my body, shrouded by my anger.*

My second marriage came to an end. It was an amicable separation. We agreed to keep the focus on our four-year-old daughter in the hopes of making the experience as good as we could for a child. We promised to never speak badly of one another to her or in front of her. As a precaution, we brought her to a divorce therapist for children. All went well, and I got to see my daughter as often as I wanted and could.

Before I knew it, I was in a new relationship. The spiritual work was producing positive results. I was feeling good. Newfound emotional maturity and spiritual growth opened me up to a new world. Life felt lighter and easier, and I was enjoying it for the first time. My new love was adventurous and curious and had a positive attitude. I felt a freedom, a lightness of being, and a sense of happiness. I was comfortable in my skin and at ease around her. I found myself walking down the street smiling on a sunny day, much unlike my old self.

However, it didn't take long for my ego, shortcomings, and insecurities to come to the surface. In time, my character flaws flogged me and my jealousy tossed me around like a rag doll. At first, I either lashed out in anger or turned quiet, cold, and distant. I either became insanely enamored or insouciant. Whatever state I fell into,

I was consistently distrusting, reactive, and rude toward most men *and*, at times, my new partner, suspecting both them and her of infidelity.

But now, having a spiritual discipline, I was keenly aware of my flaws and the harm I was causing. So, I went to God, Gerry, and the practice of restraint. Without having my old friend anger to fall back on, without being able to accuse and attack my partner or other men, my fears ferociously surfaced. They were frightening. Gerry strongly suggested I face them head-on.

He claimed I was ready to do this and encouraged me not to run away from them. Although sitting with my fears was unlike anything I'd done before, I was motivated and driven by one simple belief—I felt as though I were on the cusp of change, and I didn't want to destroy my chance of a good life. I had a glimpse of what it was like to be in a blissful, monogamous, romantic relationship, and this was the impetus compelling me to confront everything that pushed up against me.

Gerry guided me and helped me confront the fears that my anger used to keep me from feeling, acknowledging, and facing. At social gatherings, when I saw the men who I had suspicions about, I would sit quietly in my unease. I would fake being nice, polite, and friendly, as Gerry recommended. I was basically doing the opposite of everything I wanted to do. I wanted to be distant, standoffish, and curt. It was clear to me now that in the past, I would go to anger as a way to avoid fear because it was much easier to feel anger than to feel fear. Fear was unfamiliar and uncomfortable to me. But I trusted Gerry. So, I sat in great discomfort.

One evening, my partner and I attended a birthday party at a club for a guy with whom she was friends, a friendship that sparked jealousy in me. Nevertheless, I was making attempts to trust her. While entering the party, fear flooded over me. I felt as though the air was thick and weighing heavy on my body. When I walked, I felt resistance, as if I were moving in slow motion in some surreal, syrupy substance. I was hyperalert, scoping out every facial expression and bodily move in the room. Socializing was awkward at best. All my senses were buzzing. It was like an out-of-body experience. I was inundated with waves of bewilderment. There was nothing familiar to latch on to, nothing concrete. But somehow I found the strength to sit in my distress and confusion.

As the weeks went by, experiences like that got more intense and worrisome. I started hallucinating. My fears took the form of both visual and auditory hallucinations. Men who were suspects of my jealously haunted me. Their names would repeatedly pop into my head, and their images would appear in my mind and in the reflection of mirrors. I could not escape them. I found little sleep. I shook some nights, jumping out of bed at times from fright and panic. I made up excuses, telling my partner I was having panic attacks about work. I felt as though I were on the verge of insanity. I thought of leaving her, but something deep down was telling me not to run away from this struggle. Besides that, I had Gerry encouraging me to stay on the spiritual path and face my demons. He knew about my hallucinations, but no one else did. It would have been unwise to tell anyone about them anyway, especially my partner. Gerry advised me not to tell her about my hallucinations, nor share my crazy thoughts and feelings of jealously with her. "Why upset her?" He made it clear. "We work with your crazies, Carl. There's no reason to dump them on her or anyone else." I trusted Gerry and followed his instructions.

Fear was having a field day with me, manifesting itself wherever it could. I was growing weary. I wanted to cut loose from this crippling condition. I wanted to run. But I knew my go-tos were no longer options. Indeed, I had unknowingly spent my whole life running from fear, never facing it, and never getting down to the heart of it. Whenever I was faced with a challenging situation, my fight-or-flight response kicked in and I would escape the fear by going straight to anger and aggression. This made me feel like a lion, powerful and protected. Now I felt unguarded and susceptible. My fears felt disenfranchising, terrifying, disabling, debilitating, paralyzing, and immobilizing. But I no longer had a choice in the matter—how could I knowingly continue to run from fear and live with myself? No, I had to face them now; deep down, I knew it.

Facing Fear

My understanding of fear was nonexistent. Essentially, I was ignorant. Fear had been a stranger to me, lurking in the basement and hiding in the shadows. It was an unsettling feeling in my body, shrouded by my anger. It was the awesome energy that kept me perpetually uneasy. Whenever I felt criticized, pushed, attacked, unsafe, or vulnerable, I would strike back in anger before I could feel fear or acknowledge it. But now Gerry was asking me to take off my armor, lay down my sword and shield, and face the unknown. All I could do was surrender and pray for strength and guidance.

Sadly, few of us have a rich understanding of fear. As a result, we never learned how to deal with it. Take a moment to look back into your childhood. Did your parents teach you how to handle fear? Did they explain to you what fear was? Did you learn about it in school? Were any coping mechanisms given to you in the classroom? Did your church, temple, or mosque offer you tools? If your answers are no, you are not alone. As youths, my friends and I had only television, movies, and adult role models (who had little guidance themselves) to inform us. Regrettably, none of us had any interest in reading books. We were street kids; it wasn't cool. Little did we know that the wisdom is in the books. In light of this lack of guidance and good modeling, most of us were doomed to fall victim to unhealthy and unsound survival strategies. We were, in effect, destined to scramble for the most accessible thing that would comfort us when crippling fear and anxiety arose during adolescence. In Western culture, alcohol, pot, and pills were, and still are, how most of us cope with fear and anxiety. In my view, fear is the primary reason we have a large population of alcoholics and drug addicts. Fear makes us fidgety, agitated, and vexed, and so we crave quick relief. "We're feel-good junkies," as Gerry often put it. And unrealistically, we want to feel good all the time.

Some of us obsessively and vigorously work out at the gym, burning off the adrenaline, outrunning the tiger on the treadmill, as it were. More than that, physical exercise releases dopamine (a feel-good chemical), which sends signals to the brain's pleasure centers, which partly explains why the fitness industry is booming. For sure, physical exercise is by far a healthier way to de-stress than alternatives like smoking pot, drinking alcohol, or popping pills. Nevertheless, working out is only a temporary fix.

To illustrate what I mean: Years ago, early in my Yoga practice, I remember arriving at the studio overworked, overloaded, and out of sorts. Magically, ninety minutes later, I'd leave in a post-workout glow. Life was good. I was happy. But something would inevitably happen. I'd end up in a traffic jam and in a panic, frantically trying to make it to my appointment on time. Undoubtedly, exercising and staying active are necessary for good physical and mental health. But until we work on our response to stress and fear, it will slowly wreak havoc on our well-being, in spite of a physical discipline.

We may flee our fears by overeating, consuming alcohol, smoking, seeking sex, or plugging into our devices. We cleverly put a lot of effort into circumventing our fears (though most of us don't realize it). We turn the radio on as soon as we get in the car, play electronic games on the train, and turn the television on without delay once we arrive home. We schedule luncheons, arrange dinner parties, plan social events, attend concerts, go to movies, frequent nightclubs, vacation, daydream, and fantasize. We fill up the space in our lives to avoid being with ourselves and our fears. The amount of energy we expend deflecting fear is immense.

Nhat Hanh speaks on the subject, seeing it as the "practice of consumption":

We want something to cover up the pain, the sorrow and the fear and the anger in us we don't want to come up. That is why we suppress them by consuming. There is some feeling of loneliness, fear, depression inside we don't want and that is why we practice consuming. ... We do everything in order not to be—in order to avoid confronting ourselves, our real self, and this is the practice of running away.[147]

Equally important is the alarming number of people who develop mental illness, such as depression, due to chronic stress.[148] Many adopt eating disorders like anorexia or bulimia. Countless others gravitate toward gambling, pornography, or prostitution. Many of us foster quirky habits, compulsive routines, and superstitions to keep stress and anxiety at bay. We double-check, triple-check, knock on wood, make the sign of the cross as we pass a church, and carry a lucky rabbit's foot when boarding a plane. These behaviors exemplify magical thinking. Surely, impulsive and compulsive behaviors are born out of fear. Such was the case with me.

As I mentioned earlier, it was the shock of my parents' heart attacks that set the wheels in motion for my OCD. As a way to cope with the trauma and the crippling fear and anxiety it produced, my mind morphed, as it were. Out of necessity, my body channeled the fear-based thoughts of living in a chaotic world and created rituals in an attempt to control my environment. As my mental illness progressed, my ritualistic behaviors turned paralyzing. But since getting sober and developing a spiritual way of living, my OCD symptoms have miraculously minimized. Yes, at times, resisting rituals and letting go of obsessive thoughts can be burdensome, but acknowledging and admitting my powerlessness over the recurring thoughts and repetitive behaviors lightens my load. Accepting and surrendering my

OCD to a Power greater than myself eases my body and quiets my mind. When I am in the light, I obsess less and I am not nearly as compulsive. And what helps me stay in the light is a daily Yoga practice, meditation, and prayer. They keep me balanced, relaxed, rational, and less likely to get caught up in heated emotions. And they distinctly deliver me from ruminating on every thought and storyline.

Fear takes on many forms, with worrying being the most prevalent. Many of us know that worrying about someone or something doesn't affect the outcome. Yet, even with this knowledge, we can't seem to stop ourselves. In fact, most of us spend a good portion of our lives worrying; it's more common among families than we care to admit. "Oh, the weather is bad; I hope he makes it home safely from his flight." "I hope Mom is okay; she's not answering the phone." We worry about paying the bills, the important meeting we have scheduled, whether our daughter is going to be accepted into the college she wants to attend, and the test results from the doctor's office. We worry a lot. We can't resist; the urge and the pull are too strong.

As we get older, many of us turn into our parents—worrywarts. "Oh, I'm just like my father; I get nervous when the kids go to the city at night." We sit restlessly at home while our children are out having fun, staying up into the wee hours until they return safely. Then we justify our feelings by saying, "Well, I'm just being a mother; I'm supposed to worry," not realizing that our worry has less to do with loving and caring for our children and more to do with our irrational fears. The truth of the matter is, we worry about everything, not just our children. We live with anxiety and scarcely experience calm. Yes, we're able to get some rest once the kids are in bed sleeping, but as soon as we wake up in the morning, fear takes hold of us again and we're back to the same old, same old.

Strange as it seems, there are cultural components to contend with when it comes to this subject as well. Worrying is not only accepted, it's expected. If we're not visibly upset, we are often viewed as apathetic or indifferent. The standard is simple: If we're not worrying, it means we don't care. Worrying is "normal." That is, until it becomes overwhelming, consuming, and debilitating.

No doubt, fear is behind all our worry. We feel as though something bad is going to happen at any moment, though there is no real evidence of it—as I mentioned earlier, fear is false evidence appearing real. In *Alcoholics Anonymous: The Big Book*, it is no coincidence that fear is described as such: "This short word somehow touches about every aspect of our lives. It was an evil and corroding thread; the fabric of our existence was shot through with it. It set in motion trains of circumstances which brought us misfortune."[149] That's quite a description. Indeed, such a nefarious definition deserves investigation.

To begin, some fears (or phobias) are more common than others, yet they are usually unique to each individual's past experience. Among them are the fear of heights, falling, drowning, flying, spiders, the sight of blood, needles, and dismemberment. There is also the fear of saying or doing the wrong thing, making a mistake, failure, and waiting for the other shoe to drop. And let us not forget the fear of abandonment and loneliness. Fear compels us to overprotect our children. Fear impedes us from quitting the job we hate. Fear stonewalls us from leaving our abusive partner. Fear drives us to drink too much, pushes us to work out at the gym more often than we should, and coerces us to spend less time relaxing, creating, and engaging with our friends and family.

However, there are also universal fears, fears that stoke the flames that generate and fuel worry. These fears exist in all of us to one degree or another. Yet most of the time we're not consciously thinking about them. For sure, they are not always evident, but the anxiety they cause is incessantly visceral. They are why we often feel edgy, irritable, and uneasy. They are responsible for our superstitious and ritualistic behaviors. They ignite feelings of dread. And they are the cause of our existential angst and the underlying force behind all our troubles. These universal fears are the fear of aging, sickness, death, loss, and irrecoverable consequences, and they are born out of the Five Remembrances (see Chapter 5). Left unexamined and untreated, they will disable us, which is why we should heed the Buddha's advice and meditate on them. After all, there is no way to escape these universal fears, for we are powerless over them, just as we are powerless over what is, the laws of nature—God. You see, these universal fears and God are two sides of the same coin. We work with our fears, surrender to them, and accept them to get closer to God. But at the same time, we surrender to God to gain the guidance and resolve to do this and hence overcome these fears and find peace with them. Gerry would often say, "No God, know fear. Know God, no fear."

Spiritually speaking, surrendering to, accepting, and embracing these fears enables us to transform them and transcend them, allowing us to become one with God and therefore suffer less.

Nevertheless, sometimes professional help is equally necessary. Through the guidance of a therapist, we can reflect on our personal history and perhaps discover something in the past that negatively impacted us. Although trauma can certainly occur at any age and turn our lives upside down, more commonly, difficulties in adult life usually stem from early childhood trauma. Moreover, scientific findings in the field of epigenetics are showing that trauma can be biologically passed down as well.

The aforementioned Rachel Yehuda is a pioneer in this field. Her findings demonstrate that trauma can change how our genes function. Which is to say that although a personal trauma cannot change the gene code itself, it can alter the genetic programming or gene expression. Further, this genetic resetting can be biologically transmitted "through the act of reproduction."[150] Still, we are not confined to the effects of trauma, genetically inherited or otherwise. Yehuda says, "We're just starting to understand that just because you're born with a certain set of genes, you're not in a biologic prison as a result of those genes—that changes can be made to how those genes function."[151]

Whether we are genetically predisposed to the effects of trauma or not, our upbringing certainly plays a role in how we experience fear and anxiety. An example of this would be the intergenerational traumatic effects of the worrying parent.[152] Generally, a parent's fears (which were likely passed down to them) manifest into unintentional and uncontrollable urges, and they unknowingly unleash their forebodings onto their children. "Please be careful. Drive safely, and call me when you get there. You know how I worry about you." These expressions of concern were conveyed quite often at home during my upbringing. My mother lived with terrible anxiety. It may have derived from my father's heart attack; I don't know. But what I do know is that fear and anxiety were undeniably passed down to me and my siblings. Fortunately, by the time I became a parent, I was sober, and I knew that I didn't want to raise my child the same way. I wanted to end the cycle. But I had a lot of work ahead of me.

The Courage to Change

In order to change we have to pay attention more closely to ourselves and our behaviors. As an example of this, I remember a time I traveled to visit my daughter, who was living with her mom after the divorce. My daughter was expecting me that afternoon. I rang the bell, and she ran down the stairs and excitedly opened the door to greet me. I looked at her and said, "You didn't ask who it was before you opened the door. You know that you need to ask who it is first." Her face dropped from delighted to disappointed. I wanted to go on; instead, I hugged her and said, "Okay, just remember next time." Still, my strong urges taunted me to go on about it, pressing me to remind her again and again to be more careful and the importance of not making Dad worry about her. But I knew that this was fear gripping me. I knew that it was my compulsion to repeat the pattern of my upbringing. Thankfully, I didn't succumb to the urge. I let it go. The unself work was working.

Gaining a deeper understanding of what triggers us and exploring healthier ways to cope with fear and stress can be slow and demanding. Positive change and healing are a long-term commitment. Fear-based negative patterns of behavior become embedded in our brains and body. We cannot expect to get rid of them overnight.

The truth is, we can't control our environment and we can't control people, not even our kids. So, we must stop trying to run the show. "If my kids would just listen to me and do what I say, I wouldn't have to worry about them." "If people would just do the right thing, the world would be a better place. If they would simply be thoughtful, polite, considerate, and honest, we would all get along well." This was how I once was. Again and again I would get frustrated, disappointed, and angry with people and situations. I couldn't see that I was foolishly trying to control my surroundings out of fear. I was trying to create order out of chaos to dispel fear and create calm. We want people to act appropriately. We wish them to reform. But to our dismay, they seldom do. Moreover, we want them to be consistent. Inconsistency and unpredictability in people make us uneasy and throw us off-balance. In short, we want to feel in control, because acknowledging that we are not means facing our fears and, hence, reality.

So what are we afraid to face? Is there something in particular sustaining all our anxieties and worries? Well, if we were to look behind the curtain, so to speak, we would discover what is pulling the levers—death. Indeed, "the idea of death, the fear of it, haunts the human animal like nothing else."[153] It drives us to procreate. It stokes us to protect one another. It inspires us to create art, write stories, and build monuments and cities. And it charges us to destroy.

163

Be that as it may, if we are to suffer less, we will have to face all our fears, including death.

On Death

Anything can happen at any time. Death could be around the corner. Acknowledging this fact can generate immense fear and anxiety—which makes it easy to understand why we wouldn't want to think about death, never mind meditate on it, as the Buddha proposes in the Five Remembrances: *I am of the nature to die. There is no way to escape death.* So why give it any thought? Why not just wait and deal with it when it comes? Well, again, the primary reason is that death "haunts the human animal like nothing else."[154]

Like life, death is always present. Whether we are thinking about it or not, the mere *knowing* of our mortality conjures up a certain level of fear. So we try our best to duck and dodge it, although usually we do this subconsciously. At the same time, we are imperceptive of an important reality—that by pushing away death, we are pushing away life, on the grounds that life and death cannot be separated. We want life yet not death. Here lies the crux of our greatest fear.

The laws of nature have a funny way of showing up when we least expect them, and *boom!* the jig is up. We get blindsided by a potentially fatal illness or the death of a loved one. Unprepared to deal with it, we become overwhelmed, floored, or immobilized. And our walls of denial come crumbling down, because they were built on nothing more than artifice.

Painfully, I have witnessed the death of a loved one devastatingly destroy people, sending them on a downward spiral. I have helplessly watched them settle into a state of despair, unable to move on, stuck in a sort of internalized, perpetual grieving. I have watched them hold onto their pain much longer than they should have in an effort to keep the memory of their loved one burning bright, unwilling to let go.

Undoubtedly, grieving over the loss of a loved one is natural and necessary. We must mourn our loss and express our sorrow. But holding onto our grief causes us to suffer, which prolongs the pain and prevents us from experiencing happiness. As fearful as it may be, we need to feel our sadness and tenderness and face our painful feelings; we cannot deny them or control them. We must speak about them outwardly in a healing and empowering way, without the concern of seeming weak. By allowing ourselves to experience what is natural— grief and mourning—we slowly release our heartache.

There's a sadness that comes when we pine for the past, wishing that we could experience it again. We ache to be with our loved ones who are no longer with us. A state of homesickness grows, a wistfulness, a yearning to return to bygone days. Spending time in the past is antithetical to mindfulness and being present. Yet our natural leanings are to keep the past alive. We daydream and hunger for the past. But more often than not, in the course of driving down memory lane, we inevitably pass through old neighborhoods and sadness and longing slow us down.

The self wants to cling to the past. It holds on tightly, not wanting to surrender to what is. The self doesn't want to let go. In essence, it doesn't want to accept change and death. As it happens, death is not the problem. The self is the problem and the self's resistance to death. The self has this mental habit of wallowing in the past, which is why the spiritual practice of letting go is essential. Life is in the *now*; memories are not. If we desire to suffer less, we must practice letting go. By doing so and accepting what is, our pain transforms into compassion and gratitude.

When a memory arises, don't dwell on it; don't hold onto it; let it pass freely. Now you might ask, "So I should forget about my caring and nurturing grandmother and grandfather who are now deceased?

That's disrespectful and coldhearted, isn't it?" Of course we needn't forget about our past and our loved ones who are no longer with us. What I'm suggesting is that when the memory of them comes, we let it touch us lightly and then let it go, just as we do with the thoughts that arise in our seated meditation practice. When thoughts of our deceased loved ones come to mind, instead of permitting ourselves to be swept away by them, we acknowledge them and feel the emotions that may also arise. Then we lovingly let the memory go with a soft smile, allowing the thoughts and feelings to float away. We detach with love and go to gratitude for having had those people in our lives. If the memories are upsetting or disturbing and we find ourselves getting fearful, angry, or resentful, we do the same (perhaps sans the soft smile). Then we redirect our attention. In time, with practice, the memories will simply slide off the banks of the brain, bringing us back into the *now*.

When we deny what is and stuff down our fears, "they fester and undermine our entire outlook on the world. The effort to make them disappear with positive affirmations is as futile as trying to keep the waves from lapping against the shore of a lake."[155]

And so we return to the Five Remembrances: *I am of the nature to die. There is no way to escape death.* By meditating on this, we are not trying to understand the inevitable; we are embracing it. Death is not the enemy. Death is natural. And contemplating it can remind us of how fragile we are, delivering immense gratitude for each day we have on earth. By accepting death, we are accepting life, and we are fully embracing life on life's terms. In contrast, denying death causes a considerable amount of trepidation. It supports our restlessness, worry, anger, cravings, and addictions.

As a child, I was surrounded by ailing, elderly relatives. I witnessed sickness and death at a young age due to the fact that my parents had me late in life. This, and my earlier mentioned childhood trauma, led to an obsession with death. I ruminated over death and the inevitable loss of my loved ones for many years. This incessantly conjured up feelings of dread. As a means to circumvent the pain, I latched on to the first thing I could find: alcohol and drugs—which, in part, led me down a dark road toward alcoholism and depression.

But thank heavens, I got sober and clean. As a result of the unself work, my depression dissipated and my views and feelings shifted. Yes, I still think of death every day, but in a serene way, not in a fixated, frightful way as before. Death no longer stirs up fear and anxiety in me. Rather, it reminds me of how lucky I am to be alive. It drives me to cherish every moment. Nhat Hanh aids us in seeing that death is a part of life and need not be feared. Let these beautiful words be a comforting contemplation:

Some waves on the ocean are high and some are low. Waves appear to be born and to die. But if we look more deeply, we see that the waves, although coming and going, are also water … . Enlightenment for a wave is the moment the wave realizes it is water. At that moment, all fear of death disappears.[156]

Transforming Fear

What if we were to look at fear differently? What if fear wasn't the problem but simply a symptom, signal, or sign? Suppose that fear had our best interests at heart. Unquestionably, fear exists for a reason. It is there to tell us something, to help us, to inform us. Perhaps the problem is that we are not listening, that we are instead pushing our fears away or wishing them away. I suggest we stop fighting our fears, stop ignoring them, and look at them closely, listen to them, feel them, and try to understand them. I strongly believe they want our attention and that we should let them have their say.

Fear is a warning sign, an opportunity for growth, not a problem in and of itself. The fact is, fear is not the problem; we are the problem. We have always been the problem. If there is any fight at all, it is not against fear, it is against the self. Yes, the self is the problem; the self that wants to be in control, the self that wants to evade fear, the self that resists, pushes back, and is unwilling to accept aging, sickness, death, loss, and the consequences of our actions. Put simply, we must unself. That is to say, we must get rid of our self-centeredness. Once we understand this, we can begin to get curious and set about working with our fears so that, in time, our fears will become more visible and far less frightening.

This shift in perspective can profoundly change our outlook on an unexpected illness, leading us to a place where we view sickness as a wake-up call rather than a fearful foe to fight off. We might ask questions like "Why am I ill?" "Have I been getting enough sleep?" "Am I too stressed?" "Am I eating badly?" "Am I drinking too much?" Our diagnosis may be the result of a mental or emotional disturbance. Whatever the case, from this distinct frame of mind, our discovery of an illness and the fear it evokes will advance to a gentler response rather than an aggressive one. In turn, our choice of treatment may be more of a holistic one. James Gordon affirms, "Illness is not our enemy. … This is part of life, and all of life is our great teacher."[157] Yes, and fear is a part of life as well. It is not the enemy—it is our great teacher.

To be clear, it's not that we won't ever experience fear, it's that we'll no longer be afraid of it. In his book *Fear: Essential Wisdom for Getting Through the Storm*, Nhat Hanh shares his wisdom. He reassures us that we have the strength to face fear, transform it, and prevent it from controlling us. But we must sit with our fear, acknowledge it, feel it, and look fully at its causes.

We just acknowledge gently that it is there. This brings a lot of relief already. Then, once our fear has calmed down, we can embrace it ten-

derly and look deeply into its roots, its sources. Understanding the origins of our anxieties and fears will help us let go of them. Is our fear coming from something that is happening right now, or is it an old fear, a fear from when we were small, that we've kept inside? When we practice inviting all our fears up, we become aware that we are still alive, that we still have many things to treasure and enjoy. If we are not busy pushing down and managing our fear, we can enjoy the sunshine, the fog, the air, and the water. If you can look deeply into your fear and have a clear vision of it, then you really can live a life that is worthwhile.[158]

Looking directly at ourselves is a fearless action. It is difficult. Most of us, often unknowingly, diverge, distract, and deflect our emotions as a way to avoid the unease. We tune out because we're utterly uncomfortable being with our anxieties and fears. But if we want to suffer less, we will need to quiet down and feel our feelings and welcome them. We will need to sit with our restlessness. However, there is a resistance that takes place, perhaps even on cellular level. Trungpa gets to the heart of it:

Openness seems demanding and energy-consuming. ... It is uncomfortable to feel so real, so you want to numb yourself. You look for some kind of anesthetic, anything that will provide you with entertainment. Then you can forget the discomfort of reality. People don't want to live with their basic rawness for even fifteen minutes. ... That is quite challenging in ... the world of neurotic comfort where we use everything to fill up the space.[159]

As for me, in order to gain the strength and wherewithal to sit still, quiet down, and make space for my fears to come up, I had to surrender to a Power greater than myself. I had to have Gerry's support and guidance. Only then could I relax with my fears and reside in the discomfort of my disappointments, heartbreak, and hurt. Only then could I let my fears be heard.

As I chose to sit with my fears, my understanding of fear flourished, as if the forces of the universe cracked opened the floodgates. Memories started surfacing, showing me the role fear played in my life. The past took on a new shape. One of the first moments of clarity came while looking back to the time I was a budding musician. A friend of mine argued that I could never make a living as a musician. He said I was being unrealistic. I remember getting angry, although I didn't admit this to him. The feeling stayed with me for years, alongside the mantra "I'll show you."

Why did I get so bothered by his remark and opinion? Was I hurt? Was my ego bruised? His comment certainly ignited my competitive spirit, which drove me to prove him wrong. In fact, this spirit motivated me to accomplish many things over the years. But it wasn't a healthy spirit; it was ego-driven. Nevertheless, the underlying force or energy behind my "I'll show you" attitude was fear.

With hindsight, it is evident that when my friend told me I could never make a living as a musician, I got angry to avoid the fear that arose in me, for it was too fierce to bear and too frightening to face: "Maybe he is right! Maybe I'm not good enough, talented enough, and smart enough." The prospect was terrifying, so I immediately went to anger. Essentially, he kicked me in the gut and rattled me. He challenged my desires, causing me to view my dream, if only for that moment, as a pipe dream.

By practicing restraint instead of jumping to anger, we strengthen the habit of staying with the fear. By pausing, we can recognize the fear, watch it, and feel it in our body. With practice, we can change our habitual go-to response toward anger and cultivate an awareness of that gap between the catalyst and contempt (or the snappy comeback). If we sit with our fears and work with them, the anger they produce dissipates. In turn, the energy of fear will work for us, not against us.

Again, our fears are there to tell us something important. They push us out of our comfort zone, drives us to meet our goals, and propel us to change our behaviors, but they also prevent us from taking unnecessary risks and alert us to potential danger. We need to listen. For the Tibetan Milarepa, when "confronted with a gang of demons … tried every way he could to get rid of them …. He threatened them, cajoled them …. But they would not leave until he ceased regarding them as 'bad' and opened to them, saw them as they were."[160]

As for the unwanted thoughts that stir up fear in me, instead of freezing up and wishing them away, I breathe with them, calming them down. Getting bothered by them only makes them louder, bigger, and more intense. By letting them be, they dissipate and lose their power. On occasion, they tell me something. But more often than not, "sometimes a cigar is just a cigar," as the saying goes. Which is to say, sometimes a thought is just a thought—meaningless and inconsequential. Unless, of course, we attach a concern or judgment to it, which in turn can create psychological suffering. For example, "That was a horrible thought; oh my God, why am I having such a macabre thought?" The fact is, we all have random, irrational, disturbing thoughts. Unless we have a strong desire to act them out, the likelihood of possessing psychopathic tendencies is minimal, and there's little reason for concern.

Working with Gerry was paying off. I was settling into a steadier state of being, and my partner and I were feeling good about our relationship. I was feeling more relaxed. Life was good. Concerning my hallucinations, they became a part of my daily life. And to my displeasure, they eventually elected one man to represent them. Apparently fear had to attach itself to something concrete; the abstract was not enough to shake me up, I suppose. Strangely, the man was a meek soul and a friend of my partner's. His name was John. Realistically, he was the last man to worry about having an affair with my partner. Despite that, I was still apprehensive and distrustful of him on occasion. In the form of hallucinations, his image and name would come to mind regularly. It stirred up fear in me. And frankly, it frustrated me and pissed me off. Yet I had no choice in the matter; the more I wished this "bogeyman" away, the more frequently he presented himself to me—and, I might add, at the most undesirable times and places. Most notably, upon awakening after a peaceful sleep. His image even invaded my prayers, one in particular: A Prayer for Healing, the Catholic prayer, which was among my regular morning prayers that Gerry gave me. Weeks went by before I told Gerry about it. In his usual manner he gave me simple and practical advice: "Stop saying the prayer." And so I did, and continued to lumber down the path, facing these hallucinations with the hope of someday freeing myself of this farce.

CHAPTER SIXTEEN

Spirituality

My white-light experience, if I were to choose to call it that,
was more like a cataclysmic kick in the ass.

I had been hoping for a white-light experience—a light bulb going off, an aha moment, an epiphany, swift enlightenment—but it never happened. Bill Wilson and author Eckhart Tolle both had a white-light experience. Wilson speaks of literally seeing a white light;[161] Tolle does not.[162] Just the same, they both had psychic transformations in an instant. After living troubled, depressed lives for many years, a sudden shift occurred. A spiritual awakening and divine revelation took place. Their depression was lifted and they saw the world differently, as if they were seeing it for the first time.

For most of us, awakeness doesn't happen in a flash. No, it's more of a long, arduous road of ups and downs and highs and lows that seem to have no destination, deadline, or time frame. And even though we might do our utmost to arrive somewhere other than where we are, there are no guarantees. In *Light on Life*, B. K. S. Iyengar says that awakeness "arrives by the Grace of God and cannot be forced."[163]

Even after seeing the "light," Bill Wilson still struggled at times. He still had to work hard at sobriety and deepen his spirituality each day. It was a process of successes, failings, learning, and growing. He had to remain vigilant about his speech and actions. One doesn't just awaken all fixed up; no, one has to take on a spiritual way of living and do the inside work. The truth is, no matter how enlightened we are or become, we have to keep at it every day. We have to stay awake.

Understandably, this may raise the question: What is enlightenment? Well, like God, enlightenment is ineffable and must be experienced. Essentially, until we experience it, all we have is someone's word as to what it is and how to locate it. "Follow these instructions. Go outside your comfort zone. Take a leap of faith. Give up your old ways. Let go of your familiar fallbacks. Practice the spiritual principles. Surrender your ego. Trust the teachings—for a better life lies ahead." Yes, that's a lot to ask, and the prospect of change and having to surrender the self creates fear. So we hesitate, procrastinate, and often protest. In a huff, we might question the spiritual work. "What exactly is this better life that lies ahead? When will I get there? Can you guarantee me that I will get there?"

It's easy to understand why anxiety and apprehension would arise at the prospect of this undertaking, for our familiar habits, narratives, identity, and view of the world are our security blankets. Though they may not serve us well, they are familiar and comfortable, and we can count on them for better or for worse. Likewise, it is natural to doubt and distrust the unfamiliar; we want to be sure; we want to know what we are getting into; we want to know for certain that it will be worth it.

Sometimes the universe doesn't give us a choice. It eggs us on, pushes us, and eventually leaves us no other option but to change. This happened to me many times: in choosing to get sober, in surrendering to doing the spiritual work, and now with my career. When it came to my work life, things weren't going well. The great love I once had being a musician and performing withered. I was tired of touring and was turning jaded. As a result of this lack of enthusiasm, I grew unpleasant, discontent, and demanding, and I was increasingly losing work. The writing was on the wall. So, I left my career of over twenty-five years, and with it, as it turned out, my social life. There I was, without a job, without income, without my circle of friends, and without a plan.

Fortunately, I had done quite a bit of spiritual work by this time and had enough strength to cope with these significant changes, which sadly included Gerry's passing only a few months later. He had contracted liver cancer, and during surgery he had a stroke. He struggled for many months to recover through physical therapy and other medical treatments, and although he showed signs of improvement, his health ultimately took a turn for the worse. But only physically. Because as his body weakened, his faith and trust in God grew stronger and a soulful smile softened his face.

In recovery meetings, Gerry used to say, "I'm living a beautiful, sober, sane life, one day at a time in spite of myself." And you believed him, and you wanted to listen and hear what he had to say. Gerry talked the talk *and* walked the walk, and he showed me this tenfold during the last months of his life, which he spent in hospice. He had many visitors, continued to work with his sponsees and others, and inspired us all until he couldn't any longer. I have fond memories of us being together and reading the recovery literature as he serenely spoke of soon being with God. His spirit remained strong and vibrant until he physically faded into a coma during his last days.

Without my teacher and best friend, on top of the other losses, I was strangely composed. I was remarkably relaxed, sitting serenely in the depths of uncertainty and chaos. I wasn't worried about work, career, earnings, or the future. Sure, I had a small nest egg and some money to live on for a time, which certainly eased the urgency. Nevertheless, I was far from retirement. I needed to find a steady flow of income. And just as concerning, I wanted to earn a living at something I found purposeful and desirable. This was the most important lesson my parents taught me: find work that you love to do; after all, you're going to be spending a good portion of your life working.

All things considered, I thought, *I should be freaking out. I should be in a panic.* I questioned whether I had lost my mind. I nonchalantly spoke about my situation to my partner and her family. This was not something my future in-laws were particularly comfortable observing. I was unemployed and unsure what I wanted to do or how I was going to gain employment. They were concerned, to say the least. I suppose I seemed unmotivated and insouciant. My partner wanted me to at least seem driven in front of them. But I was at ease. I was expected to show a sense of urgency and alarm, but I didn't. I suppose I should have been worried, but I wasn't. Instead, I spoke about this calm state I was experiencing. I was fascinated with it, and I wanted to share it with them. So I went on speaking about it, expressing my curiosity. That is, until I realized they thought I was unhinged. *Are they right?* I thought. I began questioning myself more and more. *Am I going insane? I should be overwhelmed with worry. Why am I at ease?* Weeks went by as this strange calm stayed with me, until out of the blue, it registered. It suddenly struck me, *This is sanity.* I was actually experiencing sanity. For the first time in my life I was tasting what it was like to be sane. For sure, the spiritual work was working!

My partner couldn't compute this conversion. She would explain to others that I was reinventing myself, that it took a lot of courage for me to change my life, and that she was proud of me. I knew she was grasping for something familiar, something concrete. As for me, I was happy and in love. I was confident about this new life I was embarking on, whatever that turned out to be. A part of me knew that this was where I was supposed to be.

That said, it's not as if there weren't ideas about the future running through my head. Among other things, the thought of being a Yoga instructor came to mind. I shared this idea with my partner. She didn't seem thrilled. And days later, in a huff, she said, "I looked into it; you can't make a living being a Yoga teacher." It was evident to me she was no longer on my side. I was hurt and deflated but not angry. And this time, unlike with my past experiences in dealing with discouragement, I had a trust in a Higher Power and a *knowing*. There was fear, but there was faith. I was experiencing something different, a strength and a centeredness.

In his lecture "Looking at Fear, That Extraordinary Jewel," J. Krishnamurti addresses this experience:

> *Fear is an extraordinary jewel. ... If you can hold it and look at it, then one begins to see the ending of it. ... Fear is part of our self-centered, egotistic activity. Fear is when the ego, "the me," is isolated, when ... the self ... is separative ... that is the root of fear. ... "How can one live" you will say, "in the world without being self-centered?" ... First be free and then you will find out, not the other way round. ... It is like saying, "What is on the other side of the mountain?" You have to climb the mountain to find out. But the description of what is on the other side of the mountain is still a description. ... What we want is guarantees. "If I give this up, will you assure me of that?" And there is no assurance.*[164]

Fear can stop us in our tracks. It can keep us from climbing the mountain. There's a marvelous quote often attributed to George Addair: "Everything you've ever wanted is on the other side of fear." We must get to the other side through faith. Chödrön offers her take on this:

> *To lead a more passionate, full, and delightful life ... we must realize that we can endure a lot of pain and pleasure for the sake of finding out who we are and what the world is, how we tick and how our world ticks .... If we're committed to comfort at any cost, as soon as we come up against the least edge of pain, we're going to run; we'll never know what's beyond that particular barrier or wall or fearful thing.*[165]

Such was the case with my partner. Committed to comfort, she came up against a fearful thing—a boyfriend who was suddenly unemployed, with no immediate plan for the future. And so she ran for the hills, as it were. She wanted out quickly. I knew there was no changing her mind, so I accepted the situation.

Several days later, after gathering our things from each other's apartments, something unexpected happened. As I was leaving her place, saying goodbye, I looked at her and she suddenly started crying. As I stood there, I could see her pain. I could feel her anguish. I held her and tried to comfort her. I told her that I understood and it would be okay. Shortly afterward, I left and got into my car. I sat there and cried. But something felt different and unfamiliar. My tears were for her and her sorrow, not from my pain and hurt. I was feeling her pain. It took a moment, but I realized I was experiencing compassion, deep compassion, unlike I ever had before. In the midst of rejection, loss, and heartache, I was feeling her sadness. I had somehow stepped out of myself. I sat there in awe. I took some deep breaths. I thanked God. And then I drove away.

Within the time frame of about ten months I found myself heartbroken, out of work (with no definitive idea as to what I was going to do for a living), and still grieving Gerry's passing. The universe pulled the rug out from under me. Yes, I may have been sane and suffering far less than I would have been prior to the spiritual work, but I was far from enlightened. My partner was gone now, and I felt acutely alone. Without any sense of security or support, an unfathomable fear and a deep loneliness enveloped me. I was overwhelmed, overtaken, and dazed. I found myself in a strange land, lost, raw, and unprotected. For months I spent sleepless nights shaking in bed, sobbing, and passing out from time to time from exhaustion. There was no longer any ground beneath me. I was floating in the air of uncertainty. Nothing was solid. My perception and sense of self in the world was water-like and surreal. It felt as though every cell in my body was in a state of flux.

The relationship ended in November, and the following winter months took on a strange, dreamlike quality. When driving in my car or walking outside in the elements, the snowy terrain, the naked branches, and the frozen sky seemed to be strangely still and silent. My body and mind felt as if they were residing somewhere between life and death—but not in a morbid way, in a neutral way. I felt very much alive, yet I felt dead too. Everything was otherworldly: the air, the sights, the sounds. There was a oneness. As I moved about, my footsteps were light and the ground, the dirt, was ancient. And so, this is how it was, like I entered a timeless zone.

Thinking about it now, was I experiencing trauma? Perhaps I was, yet I wasn't guarded or triggered in any way. There wasn't a longing for all of it to disappear so I could return to my previous life and former state of being. I didn't want to go back to my old life and partner and career. No, I found myself surrendering to this new way of seeing the world, curious about where it might lead me. And this curiosity shaded the fear and discomfort I had to sit with day in and day out.

As for the hallucinations I had been having of my partner's male friend, they gradually dissipated and disappeared. But in their absence, his name repeated in rhythm in my head—*John, John, Da John, La John, John the Con, John is on.* The more I tried to ignore his name, the more my thoughts turned into the "Don't think about a pink elephant" experiment.[b] Soon after, the image of the meek man returned again. I was powerless over it. I knew it was irrational and arbitrary, but there was little I could do about it other than let it be.

I was used to having obsessive thoughts, recurring thoughts, and inner chatter and noise in my head. Actually, I didn't know what it

---

b. "The pink elephant experiment" established the paradoxical effect of thought suppression: where trying to not think of something makes it more likely to pop into your head.

was like otherwise—that's the world of someone with OCD. I was this way my whole life. But now, the thoughts and the pictures in my head were strong, disturbing, and stirring up immense frustration and fear in me. And worse, I feared they would haunt me forever and drive me mad. All I could do was surrender to the fact that I was powerless over ending this charade, and, of course, trust the process and God. Granted, I did find that proactive solutions like praying, meditating, teaching, or helping others would free me from it for a while. That said, in reality, the bogeyman was not my primary problem. I had bigger issues.

Luckily, and thankfully, I had a few friends and family who were supportive. They were a shoulder to cry on and a sounding board. But I soon felt like a burden, and deep down I knew there was nothing they could do to help me. Ultimately, I had to go through this (whatever it was) on my own; there was no way around it and no escape. Intense emotions would arise; anger toward my former employers, colleagues, and ex-partner would surface. But I refrained from acting out, immediately going to forgiveness and understanding until the anger passed. It seemed that I had developed enough trust and faith in the spiritual practice to be able to sit in the fear, anger, and pain during this difficult period. I didn't run from it. I surrendered to it. I knew I was where I needed to be. I needed to live alone, eat alone, sleep alone, and face my fears. And so I did. I sat in the uncertainty and in the sensation of groundlessness. Every day I prayed, meditated, and journaled.

I also attended recovery meetings practically every day. And in an attempt to start a new life, I gravely and fiercely made new friends, inside and outside of the recovery circle. Although I already knew the value of the recovery Fellowship, I finally understood the importance of friends, a support network, and a social life. In the past, I never made efforts to establish friendships or maintain them. My life was all about romance, sex, music, alcohol, and drugs. Granted, I had friendships, but most of them were secondary, if not incidental. This could have been due to my transient lifestyle as a touring musician, but more likely it was because of my self-centeredness and distrust of people. Whatever the reasons, my social circles were now becoming fundamentally meaningful. I sensed that life was opening up to me. Even so, I knew had a long, hard road ahead. Fear and anxiety were still sapping the life out of me.

Eventually I welcomed and embraced my current state and situation. I sensed in my core that there was something more powerful than me at work—in a hardwired way, in which the nature of my body, mind, and spirit were the driving force. Yes, it was divine intervention, although nothing magical or supernatural was at play. It was simply the Divinity within me intervening. My true nature was showing me the way and leading the way. It was a wake-up call, and I chose to answer it. Although I had little choice in the matter, my ego was pulverized and annihilated. And I was done, physically, mentally, and emotionally.

While struggling to sleep one night, twisting, twinging, and griping, I suddenly froze up. I was finished. I lay there in the dark, terribly broken and sleep-deprived. After many months of wakeful nights, writhing, weeping, and bellowing, a silence and a stillness settled over me. I collapsed in my bed, on my back, arms stretched out to the sides like a supine cross, crucified. Turning to something greater than me, I raised my hand and softly cried, "I surrender. I am done. Take my hand, God; lead the way." I let go of all my expectations and hopes. Released, my body, mind, and spirit slowly drifted into a deep, heavy sleep.

Hours passed, and the sun rose. It was quiet. I opened my eyes, and I noticed my breath. The air was crisp. Everything seemed strange, foreign, and otherworldly. The room was quiet and peaceful, as was the world outside my window. Everything had changed. My life, as I knew it, was over.

I Came to Believe

My white-light experience, if I were to choose to call it that, was more like a cataclysmic kick in the ass. A powerful force pushed me and propelled me up and over the mountain. And in the end, I emerged a different person. For sure, I came to believe in a Power greater than myself but only after surrendering to it. Once I abided by a Higher Power and experienced grace, I was convinced there was something bigger than myself. Indeed, when it comes to the spiritual world, seeing *and* experiencing is believing.

The spiritual world is not visible from the intellectual world. In other words, the spiritual realm cannot be seen from an intellectual perspective. Likewise, to the analytical mind, God is only a name and a concept. God dwells in the spiritual dimension; how can we expect to understand and experience God from the cerebral plane? We can read, study, ponder, philosophize, and debate about God and spirituality until the cows come home, but until we enter the world of the spirit, God remains invisible and unexperienced. That is to say, God remains dead, in a sense, until we surrender our will.

In theory, turning it over, trusting the universe, accepting what is, and letting God handle our problems sounds simple, but there is nothing more difficult. Yes, this I knew: I knew that I could not force my partner to stay with me and love me. I'll never forget arriving home that night we said goodbye. Falling to my knees, distraught and aching, I pleaded to God, "No, not her; not her too. I've surrendered so much to you; do I have to surrender and accept this too? Please, no, not her." I knew the answer, though; I had been on this path for far too long not to know. I knew there were no exceptions. I had to surrender what *I* wanted to what is.

I learned that we cannot expect exemptions or allowances on this path. Suffice it to say, we are free to choose any path. We can get on board with *what is* or not. We can decide to either surrender or resist. We can follow the spiritual work, or we can follow our own program. The choice is ours.

As for me, I really had no choice, especially when it came to my current situation with the bogeyman. I was growing sick and tired of his echoing name and the repetitive images in my head. In fact, my mind was growing bored of it all. As a consequence, the hallucinations went away for a while and I'd forgotten about them. Not surprisingly, and mockingly, the day I realized this, they returned. And I was back to the pink-elephant problem again. I attempted many mental games to overcome this. Among my innumerous undertakings were ignoring the hallucinations, avoiding them, discounting them, and replacing them with other thoughts and images. Nevertheless, all pursuits failed.

In time, I decided to get curious about these recurring thoughts and images. I focused on them, gave them my attention. To my amazement, I gained some insights. One was that the meek man was innocent and insignificant. In fact, he was harmless. He was never a real threat. He is actually a nice guy. In hindsight, the past hallucinations and pictures of him in my mind were symbolic. My brain seemed to have chosen that man to represent fear. And so I meditated with the intention of getting underneath his name and image to the rawness of my fears.

First Things First

Through the spiritual work, I came to realize that I didn't like God when I was younger because I didn't like myself. I was dishonest, unfaithful, and sinful in countless ways, and so how could I find comfort in a God who I could not obey and who judged me?

Gerry pointed out my egocentricities and how I was playing God. Without question, I held my lovers, friends, sources of income, and family restrictively close to me. I needed them. And out of fear of losing them, I was needy, possessive, and controlling.

Gerry used to tell me to "detach with love." But as with most everything he said, I didn't understand this at first. I only knew how to love someone insanely and possessively, or indifferently and coldheartedly; there was no healthy, middle way for me. I was either passionate or tepid, emotional or apathetic, warm or aloof. But I learned that to detach with love can only be achieved by putting something greater first. When we do this, we become compassionate, loving, supportive, autonomous human beings, and, hence, give our loved ones the freedom to grow and find their way in the world. With God, our unhealthy attachments to our friends and family wither away, freeing them from the crippling weight of our demands. When we exist without an unending craving, neediness, and dependency, truly deep and meaningful relationships can blossom. We must surrender our will and our dependencies and put a God of our understanding first. We must give love to others rather than seek it. Only then will our relationships become richer, easier, and more relaxed.

It's apparent now that I saw God as something separate from the world. He existed outside the universe and the cosmos, an Entity that sat somewhere in heaven looking down on everyone and everything. God was not a power I lacked, nor was God the laws of nature. I didn't see that all beings and all things are a manifestation of God. When I put God first and admitted my powerlessness, I flourished, as did the people in my life. I slowly became free of the bondage of self. And my daughter and loved ones became free of my smothering neediness, living their own lives outside of my small world. My heart opened up. I became useful and helpful to others.

When we unself, we are not surrendering to God for love and approval or because it is written in a religious text. We are not bowing to the *beyond* to save ourselves from God's wrath and punishment. We are not abiding to avoid being sent to hell. No, we are doing it for ourselves—so as to not live in hell on earth. We are surrendering and sacrificing our needs for the needs of others so that we may live in heaven on earth.

As Chödrön writes, "We work on ourselves in order to help others, but also we help others in order to work on ourselves."[166] This is accomplished by being a good friend, a loving partner, and an understanding parent, guide, and role model, putting our selfish desires and ego aside for the benefit of all. We don't say, "Once I overcome my depression and emotional pain, I will be free to give to others and contribute to the world" or "Once I get my head straight and find some peace and happiness, I will have the time, energy, and strength to help myself and others." Put another way, the truth is not that *once we believe in ourselves, we can change our lives.* The truth is that *if we change our lives, we will begin to believe in ourselves.*

Upon waking in the morning, we can put first things first and go to prayer and surrender. Then we can go about our day walking the spiritual path and doing the unself work.

And What of Happiness?

The wisdom of unselfing was what I returned to over and over when it came to my recurring visions of the meek man. I continued to meditate and drop any hope or expectation of the hallucinations ever going away. Soon, they turned less bothersome. Then came the morning I woke up to the image of my nemesis, hearing an inner voice saying, *This is fear! Why are you not feeling the fear? Stop analyzing; feel the fear underneath the appearance of the bogeyman. Feel the fear in your body. Of course,* I thought. *I've been so distracted, concerned, and annoyed by the intrusive thoughts, I've neglected to feel the fear.* And so, whenever the thoughts came forth, I sat with the sensation of fear.

Presently, the thoughts and form of the meek man in my mind, the hallucinations and the heartbreak, have faded. They have blended in with all my other traumas, becoming just another part of my past. The smoke cleared and the dust settled down onto the bottom surface of my mind with the rest of my memories. That's how it seems to work, provided we let go of our storylines and resentments and confront our fears, the memories become less salient. They never go away, they never disappear, but they lose their power and quiet down. Nonetheless, we must be watchful, for a mighty wind might kick them up again.

As we do the spiritual work, our thinking clears and our stresses soften. We come to be in tune with our body, mind, and heart. Our focus shifts to the personal/inner experience of the sacred. Our gut speaks to us, and we listen. God speaks to us, and we abide. We *know* what is right. That is to say, "What used to be the hunch or the occasional inspiration gradually becomes a working part of the mind."[167]

However, we must remain vigilant, for "It is easy to let up on the spiritual program of action and rest on our laurels. We are headed for trouble if we do …. What we really have is a daily reprieve contingent on the maintenance of our spiritual condition."[168] Gerry used to use the image of an escalator to illustrate this important point: If we rest on our laurels, it's much like walking up a down escalator. Once we stop walking up, we start moving down.

Reflecting on my past suicidal and homicidal thoughts and the images, hallucinations, and repeated sounds of rhythm and rhyme of the meek man in my mind, were these conditions related to my OCD? It is likely, because whenever I have stressful periods in my life, and I start experiencing images, rhythms, sounds, sticky thoughts, and an increase in ritualistic behavior, simply reminding myself that they are coming from my OCD brings me relief. Still, at the same time, I must immediately go to my Higher Power and pray. If time permits, I move on my yoga mat, meditate, go to a recovery meeting, or reach out to someone on the phone. Simply stated, I practice unselfing. And by doing so, I am restored to sanity, serenity, and happiness.

And what of happiness? Up until a short time ago, I thought the happiness I experienced with my ex-partner was because I'd met the right person and that the lightness of being I felt was the result of our mutual love, connection, and compatibility. Now I see I was wrong. It wasn't her. It was me. I was becoming happy. The work with Gerry had paid off. I was emerging out of my egocentric shell. I was opening up to the beauty of living. I was feeling alive and excited about the future. And my ex-partner, our relationship, as I now see it, was more of a sharing of this happiness; it wasn't because of it. I was happy, and the relationship was a celebration of this new birth, of being born again, as it were. The happiness was surfacing from within me.

So, in the end, my lover leaving me didn't steal my happiness, as I once believed it would. No, it brought me closer to it. It delivered me the truth: this happiness was coming from me.

Acknowledgments

I have many to thank for my good fortune. I am eternally grateful and indebted to Gerry H. His wisdom, guidance, determination, and compassion gifted me with a wonderful life. Gerry, I hope this book represents you well. You left us much too soon, but you are still with us in spirit.

I also owe my deepest thanks to my therapist for pushing me to attend my first recovery meeting and insisting years later that I reach out to Gerry. And to the woman who offered to meet me for my first recovery meeting, I am truly thankful for her gracious gesture.

Thank you to all my beta readers: Liz Colville, Erica Howton, Angelina Cottarelli Fulvini, Mark Vignali, Mitch Kuflik, Amanda Lehrer Nash, Robert Piliero, Rena Hecht, and Maureen Regan. Thank you, Amanda and Bob, for going above and beyond, editing and trimming the fat. Thank you, Suzanne Weyn and Maureen, for your time, expertise, and guidance. A big thank-you to Maureen for coming up with just the right title for the book!

Thank you to my accountant, finance guy, and brother-in-arms, Larry A. Kessler. Without you, I would be lost. You keep me afloat and on the straight and narrow. To all my students: Thank you for giving me the opportunity to speak openly about my experience and for letting me be me. And to Auste Kuncas: Thanks for pushing me to create an online presence and brand. And thank you for your support, enthusiasm, guidance, and expertise. To Rena, my longtime friend, confidante, and manager: Thank you for believing in me and this book.

If not for your friendship, enthusiasm, unwavering support, and unrelenting, diligent editing, this book would still be sitting on my desk.

Thank you to my wonderful editors, Andrea Vinley Converse (developmental/line editor) and Kelsey Mitchener (copy editor). Thank you to my brilliant cover designer, Kam Bains. And a great thank you to both my interior designer, Iram Allam, and proofreader, Ellen Tarlin.

Of course, I am beholden to my daughter. Her coming into being brought me to my Higher Power. Her very existence brings me immense joy, purpose, and meaning and motivates me to be a better person. *Al mio amore*, Angelina; thank you for all your love and support and for making our house a home. To my loving family, those who are with us and those who no longer with us, thank you for your love, support, and encouragement and for always being there. To my friends, you make my life bigger and better.

To all my teachers, thank you for your direction and for sharing the sacred teachings. To all the enlightened beings of the past and the present, thank you for gifting us with your divinely inspired wisdom and teachings. And to God, I am humbled and filled with gratitude; thank you for your grace and power. Thank you for my sobriety, sanity, and serenity. And thank you for the guidance and strength to complete this book. May it serve to help others.

Notes

1   Anthony de Mello, *Awareness: The Perils and Opportunities of Reality* (New York: Doubleday, 1992), 78.

2   Osho, *The Path of Love: The Myth of Self-Improvement,* Talk *#10* (OSHO International Foundation), https://s3-eu-west-1.amazonaws.com/oshonewsletter/oshonewsletter/globalenglish/may17/The-Myth-of-Self-Improvement.html.

3   Alan Watts, "Spiritual Authority" (lecture, Chicago, IL, 1971), https://www.organism.earth/library/document/spiritual-authority.

4   Bill Wilson, *Alcoholics Anonymous: The Big Book* (Mineola, NY: Ixia Press, 1939), 80.

5   "Step Ten," in *Twelve Steps and Twelve Traditions* (New York: Alcoholics Anonymous World Services, Inc., 2025), 93.

6   Eugene Peterson, "Answering God," *On Being with Krista Tippett,* podcast audio, December 22, 2016, https://onbeing.org/programs/eugene-peterson-answering-god.

7   "Step Six," in *Twelve Steps and Twelve Traditions*, 65–66.

8   Chögyam Trungpa, *Cutting Through Spiritual Materialism* (Boston: Shambhala, 2008), 81.

9   Wilfred Cantwell Smith, *The Meaning and End of Religion* (Minneapolis: Fortress Press, 1991), 123.

10 Ibid., 157.

11 Ibid., 156–157.

12 Ibid., 156.

13 William E. Paden, *Religious Worlds: The Comparative Study of Religion* (Boston: Beacon Press, 1994), 130.

14 Alan Watts, "On Being God" (lecture, New York, 1971).

15 Nahum 1:2 NIV.

16 1 John 4:8 ESV.

17 Psalm 103:8 ESV.

18 Psalm 103:8 ESV.

19 Romans 3:23 NKJV.

20 Andrew Newberg and Mark Robert Waldman, *How God Changes Your Brain: Breakthrough Findings from a Leading Neuroscientist* (New York: Ballantine Books Trade Paperbacks, 2009), 174.

21 Casey Luskin, "The Top Six Lines of Evidence for Intelligent Design," Discovery Institute, February 25, 2021, www.discovery.org/a/sixfold-evidence-for-intelligent-design.

22 Richard Dawkins, *The God Delusion*, film, 14:02, 16:40.

23 Thich Nhat Hanh's version of the Five Remembrances, Shambhala Publications, www.shambhala.com/the-five-remembrances-an-excerpt-from-alive-until-youre-dead-by-susan-moon.

24 Paula Marvelly, *Lao Tzu: Tao Te Ching*, The Culturium, May 17, 2020, www.theculturium.com/lao-tzu-tao-te-ching.

25 Dan Casas-Murray, "Tao Te Ching Verse 14: NoThing and NowHere," *The Tao Te Ching for Everyday Living*, December 26, 2019, www.buzzsprout.com/732839/episodes/2357948-tao-te-ching-verse-14-nothing-and-nowhere.

26 Quote by Carl Sagan. See Robert Lea, "Are We Really Made of 'Star Stuff' and What Does That Even Mean? (Video)," Space.com, August 21, 2023, www.space.com/we-are-made-of-star-stuff-meaning-truth.

27   Quote by Neil deGrasse Tyson, "We're in the Universe and the
      Universe Is in Us," from the History Channel's *The Universe*
      series, season one; "Beyond the Big Bang," www.youtube.com/
      watch?v=VVfykwiYE3s.

28   Alan Watts, "Not What Should Be, But What Is" (lecture,
      Philadelphia, 1971).

29   Matthew 19:21 NIV.

30   Sharon Salzberg and Robert Thurman, "Love Your Enemies?
      (Really?)," *On Being with Krista Tippett*, podcast audio, October
      31, 2013, https://onbeing.org/programs/sharon-salzberg-robert-
      thurman-love-your-enemies-really.

31   Merriam-Webster Dictionary, www.merriam-webster.com/
      dictionary/surrender.

32   Watts, "On Being God."

33   Ibid.

34   Wilson, *Big Book,* 417.

35   Wilson, *Big Book,* 85.

36   Association for Psychological Science, from *The Wall Street
      Journal,* "The Science of Prayer," www.psychologicalscience.org/
      news/the-science-of-prayer-2.html, Elizabeth Bernstein, "The
      Science of Prayer: Many people are praying now, and scientists
      say the practice may boost mental health," *The Wall Street Journal,*
      www.wsj.com/articles/the-science-of-prayer-11589720400.

37   The Serenity Prayer. Adopted by Alcoholics Anonymous.
      The origins are hazy; it could date back to Boethius, AD 500
      philosopher, although it's often credited to American theologian
      Reinhold Niebuhr, who alternately credited eighteenth-century
      theologian Friedrich Oetinger.

38   Addiction Prevention Coalition, "Understanding the Meaning
      Behind the AA Logo: Unity, Service, and Recovery,"

      https://apcbham.org/understanding-the-meaning-behind-the-aa-
      logo-unity-service-and-recovery.

39   The History, Philosophy and Practice of Buddhism, *The Three Jewels and Five Precepts*, https://buddha101.com/p_jewels.htm.

40   Sri Sri School of Yoga, "The Eight Limbs of Yoga and Why They Matter to Your Practice," https://srisrischoolofyoga.org/na/blog/8-limbs-of-yoga-ashtanga-yoga.

41   Proverbs 16:18 KJV.

42   Chögyam Trungpa, *Shambhala: The Sacred Path of the Warrior* (Boulder, CO: Shambhala, 2015), 25.

43   Rick Hanson and Richard Mendius, *Buddha's Brain: The Practical Neuroscience of Happiness, Love, and Wisdom* (Oakland, CA: New Harbinger Publications, 2025), 138, 142.

44   Kyczy Hawk, *Yoga and the Twelve-Step Path* (Las Vegas: Central Recovery Press, 2012), 38. See also Annalisa Cunningham, *Healing Addiction with Yoga: A Yoga Program for People in Twelve-Step Recovery* (Findhorn, Scotland: Findhorn Press, 2010).

45   John Lewis and Michael D'Orso, *Walking with the Wind: A Memoir of the Movement* (San Diego: Harcourt Brace and Company, 1998), 63.

46   Wilson, *Big Book*, xxvi.

47   Eugene H. Peterson, *The Pastor: A Memoir* (New York: HarperOne, 2012), 157.

48   Newberg and Waldman, *How God Changes Your Brain*, 145.

49   Matthew 26:41 NIV.

50   Wilson, *Big Book*, 83.

51   Wilson, *Big Book*, 70.

52   Trevor Haynes, "Dopamine, Smartphones, and You: A Battle for Your Time," Harvard University: The Graduate School of Arts and Sciences, May 1, 2018, https://unplugged.sunygeneseoenglish.org/wp-content/uploads/sites/31/2019/11/Domamine-PDF.pdf.

53   Bill Wilson, "The Next Frontier: Emotional Sobriety," *AA Grapevine*, Jan. 1958.

54   Ibid.

55   Ibid.

56   Acts 20:35 KJV.

57   Wilson, "Next Frontier."

58   Ibid.

59   "Step Twelve," in *Twelve Steps and Twelve Traditions*, 122.

60   "Tradition Two," in *Twelve Steps and Twelve Traditions*, 132–133.

61   "Emotion Regulation and Dysregulation," YouTube video, 3:46, 4:40, posted by "Ritvo Lab (Health behaviour Change)," November 30, 2013, www.youtube.com/watch?v=wcyZ2kXavb0.

62   Ibid., 4:55.

63   Adrienne A. Taren et al., "Mindfulness Meditation Training Alters Stress-Related Amygdala Resting State Functional Connectivity: A Randomized Controlled Trial," *Social Cognitive and Affective Neuroscience* 10, no. 12 (December 2015): 1758–68, doi:10.1093/scan/nsv066.

64   Peter H. Diamandis and Steven Kotler, *Abundance: The Future Is Better Than You Think* (New York: Free Press, 2012), 32.

65   Wendy M. Johnston and Graham C. Davey, "The Psychological Impact of Negative TV News Bulletins: The Catastrophizing of Personal Worries," *British Journal of Psychology* 88 (1997): 85–91, doi:10.1111/j.2044-8295.1997.tb02622.x.

66   James Doty, "The Magic Shop of the Brain," *On Being with Krista Tippett*, podcast audio, February 11, 2016, https://onbeing.org/programs/james-doty-the-magic-shop-of-the-brain-nov2018.

67   Newberg and Waldman, *How God Changes Your Brain*, 55–56.

68   Eckhart Tolle, *The Power of Now: A Guide to Spiritual Enlightenment* (Novato, CA: Namaste Publishing and New World Library, 1999), 19.

69   Quoted in Lynn Stoller, "Six Steps to Tame Anxiety: Meditation + Seated Poses," *Yoga Journal*, January 20, 2025, www.yogajournal.com/practice/yoga-sequences/meditation-seated-yoga-sequence-

tame-anxiety.

70 Max Highstein, *The Healing Waterfall, 100 Guided Imagery Scripts for Counselors, Healers, and Clergy*, https://guidedimagerydownloads.com/max-highstein.

71 Maria Nemeth, *The Energy of Money: A Spiritual Guide to Financial and Personal Fulfillment* (New York: Ballantine Wellspring, 1999), 154.

72 David Nichtern, "How to Meditate Through Strong Emotions," *David Nichtern* (blog), davidnichtern.com/how-to-meditate-through-strong-emotions.

73 Mark Hyman, James Gordon, and Penny George, "The Evolution of Medicine," *On Being with Krista Tippett*, podcast audio, December 3, 2015, https://onbeing.org/programs/mark-hyman-james-gordon-penny-george-the-evolution-of-medicine.

74 Adapted from James Gordon.

75 Gordon Hempton, "Silence and the Presence of Everything," *On Being with Krista Tippett*, podcast audio, May 10, 2012, https://onbeing.org/programs/gordon-hempton-silence-and-the-presence-of-everything.

76 Ibid.

77 Richard Miller, "Be Part of Something Bigger: Meditation Can Help Us Get in Touch with the Universal Life Force That Connects Us All," *Yogahood Online* (blog), May 20, 2025, https://yogahoodonline.com/be-part-of-something-bigger.

78 Ibid.

79 Ibid.

80 Ibid.

81 Ibid.

82 Ibid.

83 Bill P., Todd W., and Sara S., *Drop the Rock: Removing Character Defects; Steps Six and Seven*, 2nd ed. (Center City, MN: Hazelden Publishing, 2005), 10.

84   Trungpa, *Cutting Through*, 70.

85   Ibid., 285.

86   Ibid., 223.

87   Pema Chödrön, *When Things Fall Apart: Heart Advice for Difficult Times* (Boulder, CO: Shambhala, 2016), 39.

88   Osho, *Essence of Spiritualism* (Meerut, India: Dynamic Publications, 2006), 257.

89   Trungpa, *Cutting Through*, 189–190.

90   J. Krishnamurti lecture, California, 1977.

91   James 2:26 NKJV.

92   Derrick Jensen, "Beyond Hope," *Orion*, May/June 2006, https://orionmagazine.org/article/beyond-hope.

93   Trungpa, *Cutting Through*, 69.

94   Parker Palmer and Courtney Martin, "The Inner Life of Rebellion," *On Being with Krista Tippett*, podcast audio, January 8, 2015, https://onbeing.org/programs/parker-palmer-courtney-martin-the-inner-life-of-rebellion.

95   Joseph Campbell, *Reflections on the Art of Living: A Joseph Campbell Companion*, ed. Diane K. Osbon (New York: HarperCollins, 1991), 8.

96   B. K. S. Iyengar, *Light on Yoga: The Bible of Modern Yoga* (New York: Schocken, 1979), 19.

97   Ibid., 13.

98   Ibid., 19.

99   Yoga Health Center, *The Connection Between Yoga and Mindfulness Meditation*, https://www.yogahealthcenter.com/blog/the-connection-between-yoga-and-mindfulness-meditation.

100   Abraham H. Maslow, *Religions, Values, and Peak-Experiences* (New York: Penguin Books, 1964), 71.

101   Bessel van der Kolk, "How Trauma Lodges in the Body, Revisited," *On Being with Krista Tippett*, podcast audio, July 11,

2013, https://onbeing.org/programs/bessel-van-der-kolk-how-trauma-lodges-in-the-body-revisited.

102   Bessel van der Kolk, "Trauma and Resilience Land in Our Bodies," *Becoming Wise*, podcast audio, July 25, 206, https://onbeing.org/programs/trauma-resilience-land-bodies-bessel-van-der-kolk-2.

103   Richard Davidson, "A Neuroscientist on Love and Learning," *On Being with Krista Tippett*, podcast audio, February 14, 2019, https://onbeing.org/programs/richard-davidson-a-neuroscientist-on-love-and-learning-feb2019.

104   Hanson and Mendius, *Buddha's Brain*, 18.

105   St. Thomas and Area AA, *A.A. Acronyms*, https://aastthomasarea.org/a-a-acronyms.

106   Gavin de Becker, "Living with Violence," *Waking Up with Sam Harris*, podcast audio, August 6, 2017, www.samharris.org/podcasts/making-sense-episodes/90-living-with-violence.

107   Friedrich Nietzsche, *Thus Spake Zarathustra: A Book for All and None* (New York: The Macmillan Company, 1896), 39.

108   Amanda Beltrani, *What is Catharsis?*, Palo Alto University, https://paloaltou.edu/resources/business-of-practice-blog/what-is-catharsis.

109   Brené Brown, "The Power of Vulnerability" (lecture, TEDxHouston, June 2010), www.ted.com/talks/brene_brown_the_power_of_vulnerability.

110   Judith Herman, *Trauma and Recovery: The Aftermath of Violence—From Domestic Abuse to Political Terror* (New York: Basic Books, 1997), 158.

111   Ibid.

112   Van der Kolk, "How Trauma Lodges in the Body, Revisited."

113   Bessel van der Kolk, "How Trauma Lodges in the Body," Daily Good, October 20, 2017, www.dailygood.org/story/1824/how-trauma-lodges-in-the-body-on-being.

114 Rachel Yehuda, "How Trauma and Resilience Cross Generations," *On Being with Krista Tippett*, podcast audio, July 30, 2015, https://onbeing.org/programs/rachel-yehuda-how-trauma-and-resilience-cross-generations-nov2017.

115 Ibid.

116 Osho, *What is the role of therapy in meditation?*, OSHO International Foundation, *The Great Pilgrimage: From Here to Here*, Talk #27, https://www.osho.com/meditation/meditation-tool-kit/questions-about-meditation/what-is-the-role-of-therapy-in-meditation.

117 Luke 22:42 KJV. Paraphrased.

118 The Four Absolutes were first adopted by the Oxford Group in the early twentieth century from a book written by Robert Speer entitled *The Principles of Jesus*. Speer called them the Four Principles, and he believed they represented the standards and principles taught by Jesus Christ. The term *absolutes* later came from Henry B. Wright of Yale, citing Speer in his book *The Will of God and a Man's Lifework*. Frank Buchman and the Oxford Group later adopted them and called them the Four Absolutes. See https://silkworth.net/alcoholics-anonymous/the-four-absolutes-2.

119 Wilson, *Big Book*, 48.

120 "Step Ten," in *Twelve Steps and Twelve Traditions*, 90.

121 Pema Chödrön, *Don't Bite the Hook: Finding Freedom from Anger, Resentment, and Other Destructive Emotions* (n.p.: Shambhala Audio, 2007), CD.

122 Richard Rohr, *Dancing Standing Still: Healing the World from a Place of Prayer* (Paulist Press: 2014), 78–80.

123 Gaur Gopal Das (@gaurgopaldas), "When you say a sorry, it doesn't mean that you are wrong. It just means that you value the person and the relationship more than being right," Instagram post, October 18, 2021, www.instagram.com/reel/CVMnbw0o9o1.

124   Nemeth, *Energy of Money*, 200.

125   Pema Chödrön, "Bill Moyers and Pema Chödrön," *Bill Moyers on Faith and Reason*, PBS, August 4, 2006, www.pbs.org/moyers/faithandreason/print/faithandreason107_print.html.

126   Pema Chödrön, *Practicing Peace in Times of War* (Boston: Shambhala Publications, 2006), 41–42.

127   Pema Chödrön, "The Answer to Anger and Aggression Is Patience," *Shambhala Sun*, March 1, 2005.

128   Osho, *Emotional Wellness: Transforming Fear, Anger, and Jealousy into Creative Energy* (New York: Harmony Books, 2007), 270.

129   Thich Nhat Hanh, *Living Buddha, Living Christ*, 10th ed. (Toronto: Berkley Publishing Group, 2007), 103.

130   *Merriam-Webster Online Dictionary*, s.v. "passion," www.merriam-webster.com/dictionary/passion.

131   Trungpa, *Cutting Through*, 105.

132   *Merriam-Webster*, s.v. "compassion," www.merriam-webster.com/dictionary/compassion.

133   *Merriam-Webster*, s.v. "passion."

134   Thich Nhat Hanh, "Dharma Talk: Cultivating Compassion, Responding to Violence" (lecture, Berkeley, CA, September 13, 2001).

135   *Significance of Four Gates*, Wisdom Library, wisdomlib.org/concept/four-gates; "The Four Gates of Speech," Mind Body and Spirit Care, https://mindbodyandspiritcare.com/2021/10/05/the-four-gates-of-speech.

136   Thich Nhat Hanh, *How to Fight* (Berkeley, CA: Parallax Press, 2017), 123.

137   Rick Warren, *The Purpose-Driven Life: What on Earth Am I Here For?* (Grand Rapids: Zondervan, 2013), 186.

138   Bill Wilson, *Alcoholics Anonymous: The Big Book*, 3rd ed. (New York: Alcoholics Anonymous World Services, 1998), 552.

139 Wilson, *Big Book*, 61.

140 "Step Ten," in *Twelve Steps and Twelve Traditions*, 92.

141 Spiritual bypassing is a propensity to use spiritual practices and attitudes to sidestep unprocessed psychological and emotional problems. See: Diana Raab, Ph.D., "What Is Spiritual Bypassing? John Welwood, who coined the term, died this week." *Psychology Today*, May 31, 2024.

142 "Putting on the Leather Shoes...," NewBuddhist.com, https:// newbuddhist.com/discussion/24372/putting-on-the-leather-shoes.

143 Nelson Mandela, Friends of Silence, https://friendsofsilence.net/ quote/author/nelson-mandela.

144 Matthew 5:44 KJV.

145 Newberg and Waldman, *How God Changes Your Brain*, 135.

146 Kristin Strachan, "The Anger-Eating Demon," https:// kristinstrachan.medium.com/the-anger-eating-demon-81e08182c60f.

147 Thich Nhat Hanh, "Mindfulness of Anger: Embracing the Child Within" (lecture, Green Lake, WI, 2003).

148 "I'm So Stressed Out! Fact Sheet," National Institute of Mental Health, accessed September 25, 2025, www.nimh.nih.gov/health/ publications/so-stressed-out-fact-sheet.

149 Wilson, *Big Book*, 68.

150 Yehuda, "How Trauma."

151 Ibid.

152 Nagy A. Youssef, et al., "The Effects of Trauma, with or without PTSD, on the Transgenerational DNA Methylation Alterations in Human Offsprings," *Brain Sciences* 8, no. 5 (May 8, 2018): 83, doi:10.3390/brainsci8050083.

153 Ernest Becker, *The Denial of Death* (New York: Free Press, 1973), 27.

154 Becker, *Denial of Death*, 27.

155   Nemeth, *Energy of Money*, 136–137.

156   Nhat Hanh, *Living Buddha*, 138.

157   Hyman, Gordon, and George, "Evolution of Medicine."

158   Thich Nhat Hanh, *Fear: Essential Wisdom for Getting Through the Storm* (New York: HarperOne, 2012), 4.

159   Chögyam Trungpa, *Smile at Fear: Awakening the True Heart of Bravery* (Boston: Shambhala Publications, 2009), 58–59.

160   Trungpa, *Cutting Through*, 241.

161   Alcoholics Anonymous World Services, 1957.
      Alcoholics Anonymous comes of age: a brief history. New York: Alcoholics Anonymous World Services, 64.

162   Tolle, *Power of Now*, 4.

163   B. K. S. Iyengar, *Light on Life: The Yoga Journey to Wholeness, Inner Peace, and Ultimate Freedom* (n.p.: Rodale, 2005), 200.

164   J. Krishnamurti, "Looking at Fear, That Extraordinary Jewel" (lecture, Brockwood Park, England, August 26, 1984).

165   Pema Chödrön, *The Wisdom of No Escape* (Boulder, CO: Shambhala, 2018), 1.

166   Pema Chödrön, *Start Where You Are: A Guide to Compassionate Living* (Boston: Shambhala Publications, 1994), 190.

167   Wilson, *Big Book*, 84.

168   Wilson, *Big Book*, 82.

About the Author

CARL T. VREELAND is an author, musician, singer/songwriter, podcaster, and Yoga and Buddhist meditation teacher. He has studied Yoga and Buddhism with several highly regarded teachers, including Alan Finger and David Nichtern. As a musician, Carl toured with many world-renowned artists and appeared on TV shows, including Late Night with Conan O'Brien and Live with Regis and Kelly. His music can be heard on TV shows, including Anthony Bourdain's No Reservations, Jersey Shore, and The Oprah Winfrey Show. Carl's songs can also be found in such films as Trust the Man, starring Julianne Moore and David Duchovny. Carl has a daughter and lives in the New York City area.

Visit Carl T. Vreeland online at www.carltvreeland.com and on most social platforms using the handle @carltvreeland.

For speaking engagements and appearances, please contact Rena Hecht at Red Letter Events: rena@redlettereventsnyc.com.

Lauer Books LLC